D0235171

"*Messages from Margaret* is a heartfelt book that offers every reader expanded und╌╌╌nding, creative solutions, and most of all hope for the futur╌ ╌╌uminates the br╌╌ ╌╌ ╌irit!

— ╌ee Woo╌ ╌╌r, C╌S This M╌ ╌or; Ne╌ York ╌ ╌ ╌est ╌ellin╌ ╌ W╌ ╌ ╌ruff, ╌ ╌ ╌n un Instant, and author of Perfectly Imperfect and the *New York Times* best-selling novel *Those We Love Most*

---

*A short, easy guide to a spiritual awakening,
this book has something for everyone!*

— **Anthony Mrocka**, senior editor, *Evolving Soul* magazine

---

"*Bravo! Gerry Gavin is the real deal. Read **Messages from
Margaret** for words of hope and rejuvenation, and you
will realize that you never need to go through life's challenges
or triumphs alone—all you have to do is ask.*"

— **Ariel & Shya Kane**, award-winning, best-selling
authors of *How to Have a Match Made in Heaven: A
Transformational Approach to Dating, Relating and Marriage*

"***Messages from Margaret*** *will resonate with readers
in ways that they didn't realize existed.*"

— *Sedona Journal of Emergence*

"*I've witnessed Gerry channel Margaret's profound messages and
teach others how to communicate with their own angels. He is truly
authentic! He communicates these truths and messages in such a
peaceful and gentle way. I loved this book, and I know you will, too!*"

— **Karen Noe**, psychic medium and author of *Through the
Eyes of Another: A Medium's Guide to Creating Heaven on Earth
by Encountering Your Life Review Now*

"Gerry Gavin is a man of great integrity and wisdom. I am sure that *Messages from Margaret* will be a great resource to people who are looking for healing, hope, and guidance in the modern world."

— **Martin Boroson,** author of *One-Moment Meditation: Stillness for People On the Go*

"What are normally considered difficult-to-comprehend topics become very easy to understand when explained by Margaret. I found myself saying things like, "That makes so much more sense now." It's inspiring and enlightening, and for me provides a very easy understanding of who we are, where we're going, and what we're doing here. . . . I would venture to say it will help anyone who reads it with their journey as well. Great book!"

— **T Love,** host of *Energy Awareness,* BlogTalkRadio

"*Messages from Margaret* is a wonderful, wonderful book! I couldn't put it down. If you are ready to open your heart and expand your mind, you will find yourself on a journey of exploration, vision, and wisdom. You will truly connect to your higher self from Margaret's teachings and actively pursue your soul's fulfillment.

— **Dr. Pat Baccili,** host of *The Dr. Pat Show* and creator of Transformation Talk Radio: BBS Radio/Voice America

MESSAGES

FROM

Margaret

ALSO BY GERRY GAVIN

Angels and Shamans (audio workshop on CD or MP3)

Drum Music for the Shamanic Journey or Shamanic Tapping (MP3)

Personalized Guided Meditation/Self-Hypnosis Recordings
(CD or MP3)

All of the above are available at **www.gerrygavin.com**

MESSAGES
FROM
Margaret

DOWN-TO-EARTH
ANGELIC ADVICE
FOR THE WORLD
. . . AND YOU

GERRY GAVIN
EDITED BY MEGAN FINNEGAN

HAY HOUSE
Australia • Canada • Hong Kong • India
South Africa • United Kingdom • United States

First published and distributed in the United Kingdom by:
Hay House UK Ltd, 292B Kensal Rd, London W10 5BE. Tel.: (44) 20 8962 1230;
Fax: (44) 20 8962 1239. www.hayhouse.co.uk

Published and distributed in the United States of America by:
Hay House, Inc., PO Box 5100, Carlsbad, CA 92018-5100. Tel.: (1) 760 431 7695 or
(800) 654 5126; Fax: (1) 760 431 6948 or (800) 650 5115. www.hayhouse.com

Published and distributed in Australia by:
Hay House Australia Ltd, 18/36 Ralph St, Alexandria NSW 2015.
Tel.: (61) 2 9669 4299; Fax: (61) 2 9669 4144. www.hayhouse.com.au

Published and distributed in the Republic of South Africa by:
Hay House SA (Pty), Ltd, PO Box 990, Witkoppen 2068. Tel./Fax: (27) 11 467
8904. www.hayhouse.co.za

Published and distributed in India by:
Hay House Publishers India, Muskaan Complex, Plot No.3, B-2, Vasant Kunj,
New Delhi – 110 070. Tel.: (91) 11 4176 1620; Fax: (91) 11 4176 1630.
www.hayhouse.co.in

Distributed in Canada by:
Raincoast, 9050 Shaughnessy St, Vancouver, BC V6P 6E5. Tel.: (1) 604 323 7100;
Fax: (1) 604 323 2600

Copyright © 2012 by Gerry Gavin

The moral rights of the author have been asserted.

Cover and interior design: Tricia Breidenthal

All rights reserved. No part of this book may be reproduced by any mechanical, photographic or electronic process, or in the form of a phonographic recording; nor may it be stored in a retrieval system, transmitted or otherwise be copied for public or private use, other than for 'fair use' as brief quotations embodied in articles and reviews, without prior written permission of the publisher.

The information given in this book should not be treated as a substitute for professional medical advice; always consult a medical practitioner. Any use of information in this book is at the reader's discretion and risk. Neither the author nor the publisher can be held responsible for any loss, claim or damage arising out of the use, or misuse, or the suggestions made or the failure to take medical advice.

A catalogue record for this book is available from the British Library.

ISBN 978-1-78180-107-9

Printed and bound in Great Britain by TJ International Ltd, Padstow, Cornwall

For Gail Lisa . . . my love, my friend, and my greatest inspiration. I am still your biggest fan! This book would not have been possible without you.

LEISURE AND CULTURE DUNDEE	
C00683349X	
Bertrams	18/12/2012
	£10.99
ARD	133·93

"The soul at its highest is found like God, but an angel gives a closer idea of Him. That is all an angel is: an idea of God."

— Meister Eckhart

"An angel can illuminate the thought and mind of man by strengthening the power of vision."

— St. Thomas Aquinas

CONTENTS

FOREWORD

> *Written with love and*
> *gratitude for a dear friend*
> *and special angel in*
> *my life, Gerry Gavin.*

As an ordained interfaith minister for family caregiving, I have had the joy and privilege of working with and knowing Gerry Gavin for many years. We have shared our mutual journeys and ministries of love and service through family caregiving, both personally and professionally.

When I heard that he, at Margaret's urging, had written this book, I knew it would be both special and deeply real. That is who Gerry Gavin is. He is a man not afraid of asking questions, seeking, doubting, and being candid about his explorations and challenges . . . and yet, facing each, he has grown to heights of experience and expression that are rarely matched.

In *Messages from Margaret,* he begins by sharing his own journey into such a relationship . . . into the deeper spiritual quest of life and that realm of spiritual reality that's available to all who are willing to dig deeper and find greater meaning and strength. His candor about his doubts if such angelic connections were even possible, or merely fantasy and escape, immediately invites comfort for all readers in dealing with this expansion of thinking, faith, and possibilities.

Throughout my years of ministry in family caregiving, I have regularly given to persons with whom I am working or counseling lovely, small, hand-carved angels from Bali, where I also reside. *Never* has anyone—faith filled or faith averse—ever said, "*No.* Take it back!" Everyone has wanted his or her angel, for in that symbol is hope and goodness, the Divine in a form not filled with dogma, doctrine, and theology, but rather with love, support, and the words that all of us associate with angels: "Fear not."

This desire for communication between humans and the Divine is found in all religions and theologies, where angels or messengers have often been used as conduits of support, guidance, hope, comfort, perspective, and encouragement. Communication between humans and the Divine is enhanced when we come to understand that we, as children of God, are like the Creator: Divine in essence.

In *Messages from Margaret,* Gerry Gavin shares his journey of making contact with his inner Divinity. Through Margaret, from their correspondences and conversations, he begins to accept, understand, and learn from the Divine within, bringing forth this connection and sharing it with all of us.

This very eloquent and honest work is a must read for all persons wishing to expand their lives. It is a guidebook of further ways to expand the truth that we are indeed not human beings trying to have a spiritual experience, but rather *spiritual beings having a human experience.* We are, in our essence, vehicles and vessels through which the Divine can express and reveal more to the world. But to do this, we need to be willing to put aside prejudice, doubt, and fear . . . and *be still* in the presence of the Divine.

Then, using the very practical and real tools found within this book, we need to develop our spiritual eyes, ears, hearts, and minds. We need, as Gerry did, to put aside our doubts and move forward into the realm of *spiritual possibilities,* guided by our angels.

Gerry, thank you for this powerful journey into the world of the Spirit. And thank you, Margaret, for sharing with us in a manner that looks at our human limitations from a point of no limitations, only from a perspective of goodness, light, power, and love. And in that may we all find the same, and then share through service, one to the other.

As the angels said, *Fear not!* Just go ahead and read!

Rev. Gregory L. Johnson
Creator: Care for the Family Caregiver Initiative
Fellow: New York Academy of Medicine
Volunteer chaplain: NYPD Gay Officers Action League
Founding member and former Co-chair: NYC Family Caregiver Coalition
Member: National Family Caregiver Support Program Task Force, Washington, DC

CHAPTER 1

THE RELUCTANT SHAMAN

> *This was the stuff that movies were made of—moving objects, voices and apparitions, room temperatures that would vary by more than 20 degrees, and a mist that would descend the stairs or hover at the top. It was, to say the least, terrifying!*

I didn't realize it then, but this book started back in 1990, when my roommate, Gail, and I moved into a house that turned out to be haunted. I had only experienced the most basic of psychic phenomena before that time—déjà vu, sometimes a precognition of who was going to visit or was calling on the phone. But this was different. This was the stuff that movies were made of— moving objects, voices and apparitions, room temperatures that would vary by more than 20 degrees, and a mist that would descend the stairs or hover at the top. It was, to say the least, terrifying!

For the longest time I said nothing to Gail, fearful that this was all my imagination. Finally I approached her, and she happily admitted that she had been seeing and feeling things, too, and was afraid to tell me because she didn't want to look crazy either.

Not wanting to move, since Gail had just purchased the house, we began to look into everything we could find out about what was happening at our home. We read books, talked to our local pastor (who came and blessed the house from the bottom of the steps and then ran out), and finally sought the help of psychics—in whom I had dubious belief.

I had also shared the story of what was happening with a close friend, who came up with a rather curious suggestion. He had been in therapy for some time, but had recently been seeing a therapist who was also a gifted psychic. The combination of her skills had turbocharged his therapy sessions. I liked this idea because she utilized her inherited, multigenerational psychic abilities in concert with her substantial traditional psychology credentials, which made her both credible *and* gifted.

When I called my friend's therapist/psychic to ask her about the house situation, she asked me about what was happening in my house before I had a chance to tell her about it. Then she channeled a ceremony that she said would rid the house of its otherworldly pests. She explained that channeling involves opening your mind to receive information from spiritual sources, much in the same manner that artists, musicians, and writers will often refer to the inspiration of their "muse." She told me that three people needed to do the same ceremony three different times, on varying days and hours. So that was what Gail, my daughter Melissa, and I set out to do. I must admit that I went into this as a great disbeliever—until we actually did the ceremony. We knew that, essentially, what we would be doing was a form of exorcism. What we didn't know was what was going to happen.

House alarms went off for no reason, doors slammed shut by themselves, and behind the closed doors we could hear the sounds of furniture drawers opening and slamming. We even had to slowly read the text of what we were saying off of big cue cards, because our words seemed at times to come out of our mouths garbled or confused. There was banging on the walls and a sick feeling in our stomachs—basically anything that could possibly scare us into stopping. I think that if this had been a rental, we would have been on the first bus out of town—but this was *our* house. We were ready to put up a fight, and we didn't stop.

By the end of the third ceremony, the house felt better to everyone. Everyone but me! I felt physically horrible, like every ounce of strength had been sucked out of me. I felt as though I had been somewhat altered by the experience; I didn't feel like myself. Just prior to the last ceremony, Gail felt compelled to give me some AA batteries that she said I should put in my shirt pocket. She didn't know why; she just felt that it was important. When we finished the ceremony I checked my pocket, and the batteries had partially melted. I had that same effect on three car batteries over the next three weeks.

Since this was beginning to get expensive, I called back our psychic/therapist to see what was going on, and she asked me if I had followed her instruction to purchase a directional compass and if I was sure I had been standing with my back to the north during the ceremony. When I confirmed this, she explained to me that all of the negative spiritual energy that left the house had, quite literally, passed through me on its way out. She explained this after the fact, because she was sure that if she had told me beforehand I might not have felt confident (good guess) and that I might not have done it (even better guess)! She further explained that she sensed I had the spiritual strength and protection to survive this energy, and learning to recognize it would later come to help me in my work. She sensed that within two years I would meet someone who would totally change my life and would take me into a new direction and "partnership" of sorts. She said that this battle with our unwanted home dwellers would be a good experience. This did turn out to be true.

At that time, however, going through the experience made me sure of one thing: There was no way that I was going to become involved in any work that involved energy, spirits, ceremonies, or psychics. No way, no how!

That was until the fall of 1991. At Gail's urging, we decided to both enroll in massage school, her for a career change and me to have a good secondary income. Our teacher was an excellent traditional massage therapist, counselor, and instructor, but she also brought other strengths to the table. As a cross-cultural healer who had been schooled by indigenous healers in many countries, she would introduce the class to all types of folk healing traditions, and while I had promised myself that I would never again dabble in the world of otherworldly beings, I found myself opening up to more and more wondrous experiences. I became deeply fascinated with the work of indigenous shamans and began to study with other teachers and then with their teachers, learning about all of the positive aspects of humans opening up to their spiritual connection and how empowering that connection could be.

Almost two years to the day after our haunted-house psychic's prediction, I met my angel, Margaret.

It happened, as most deep spiritual experiences do, at a time of total personal surrender. I was at a really hard emotional block in my life, and I knew that I needed some heavy-duty guidance to get through it. By this point I had become fairly skilled at many shamanic practices and would regularly come into contact with spirit guides and power animals. But I had never come across an angel, and I knew instinctively that this was something I needed to accomplish. Not knowing what to do, I spoke aloud to the angel that I hoped was out there listening: "If I only knew your name, I know I could find a way to talk to you!"

I closed my eyes, and everything went white, like a blank movie screen, and then the word *Margaret* began to appear. I opened my eyes and closed them again, and the word was still there. I thought to myself, *What kind of angel name is Margaret?* I was expecting something much more celestial sounding. But now, rather than the one word filling the screen, the word began to write itself in every different font that I could possibly imagine

. . . over and over again . . . filling every inch of the white screen before my closed eyes.

I opened them again, very confused. Back then, I wasn't very fond of the name Margaret. I again asked the question and closed my eyes. This time the screen was as black as night, and the name began to again appear, but now it was in white letters on the black screen and again in every font style I could imagine and then some.

I finally opened my eyes, convinced that the angel I was seeking was, in fact, named Margaret!

In the years that preceded this event, I had learned about many types of spiritual communication, and for some reason, what felt right to reach out to Margaret at that particular time was a method called *automatic writing*. The technique is really very simple yet very powerful. You begin by writing a letter to the spiritual guide you desire. It could be to the Creator, like Neale Donald Walsch did in *Conversations with God,* it could be to a dearly departed loved one, or, in my case, to my new angel friend. You write the letter and ask advice as though you are speaking to the most loving being you know, and then—and this is the hard part—you write a letter back to yourself. In this letter to yourself, you imagine that the answer is coming from someone who deeply loves you and only wants what is best for you, and you allow that to flow.

Prior to this time, I had never tried this exercise because it seemed foolish to me. Clearly, if I was writing the letter and I was also writing the answer, then it would seem to me that I was going to get the answers that I most wanted to hear.

But when I wrote this first letter to Margaret, I found that my supposition could not have been further from the truth. I was going through a very difficult period in my life. I was struggling with a relationship, money was scarce, and it seemed like every day was one step forward and three steps back. I wrote to Margaret asking why my life seemed so hard, why my relationship wasn't working out, and why it was so hard to get ahead.

I began it with "Dear Margaret" and ended it with "Love Gerry," and then I began the response with "Dear Gerry." I closed my eyes for a moment, took a deep breath, and began writing. Her response started with a phrase that I would not think to use, and yet it is one that has begun every one of the thousands of letters I have received from Margaret since that time: "Hello, Dear One, and welcome." From there I began to write, quicker than I usually do, and the message was so different from the wording and process of how I usually think and write that I found that I was also reading it with fascination, as though it was being written by someone else. The insight as to the feelings and emotions of the person I was in a relationship with was far more perceptive and gentle than I could give myself credit for. The gentleness toward me also left me feeling as if I no longer needed to beat myself up for not being the "everything to everybody" that I was always trying to be. There was not an ounce of blame or judgment in the letter, although she managed to do this at the same time that she clearly showed me my responsibility for how I reacted to, and created, all of my experiences. I wrote and wrote and finally found myself closing the letter with what has become her signature line: "Go in peace, Love, Margaret."

I must have reread that letter 100 times, and each time I was more amazed by the love and insight that she offered. But I still was not totally convinced that this could not have been a product of my imagination.

So I decided to test the validity of the information she gave me. She shared with me the reasons that some of the people in my life reacted to me in certain ways. They were kind and gentle insights into their behaviors that I had never considered. When I called them to ask if they could have been feeling this way, to my amazement, the people in question responded with shock and wonder that I had intuited what it was that they were feeling.

I must admit that while this experience elevated my level of understanding, I was petrified to let people know that the information had come from my new pen pal—and oh, by the way, she was an angel named Margaret.

I kept writing to Margaret, almost daily for the first year. I found out that, while she could help me with insights, she would not predict the future, because that would impair my freedom of choice, which would mean that she was creating my reality and not me. She could, however, help me to understand the most productive actions I could take to create the life I desired. I found her to have a wonderful sense of humor and a great skill of being able to take very complex concepts and break them down into easily digestible tidbits that I could understand.

That sense of humor came out one day when I asked her, "Why me? What is it about me that made me special enough to be allowed to talk to an angel?" Her response was to say that there was "nothing special about me" and that hopefully people would realize that if I could do this then anybody could! She later explained that while she was having some fun with me, her true meaning was not that I wasn't special, but that all of us are equally special in our ability to communicate with angels and the Creator.

And with that she took our relationship to a new level, indicating that it was time for me to share her messages with other people. I had only shared my messages from Margaret with a couple of close friends and family members, and the concept of coming out of the "psychic closet" was really frightening. What would people think of me? What if the information I got for other people seemed like nonsense to them? Then not only would they think I was a fraud, but the fact that I thought I was talking to angels would make me a crazy fraud. She assured me that everything would be all right, and the next day I "coincidentally" got a phone call from a friend who knew about Margaret and suggested that I speak to her friend, a gifted psychic who might be able to give me some advice as to how to share this experience with others.

I went to see the psychic, and much to my surprise, when I told her my story, rather than offering me advice, she instead asked if I would do a reading for her. My hand shook as I wrote Margaret's answers to her questions. I didn't know how she would react to the information I received, since some of it pointed out areas where she was creating the conflicts in her life that she was concerned about. But the answers offered her a level of insight about herself that she had never achieved before, and she also was amazed at how kindly and gently the advice had been delivered. She immediately got on the phone to arrange for two other well-known psychics to come see me the next day, so that I could "read" for them.

I remember barely sleeping a wink that night. I was grateful that I had been able to get her information correct, but now she was calling in people who were well known for the accuracy of their predictions and who had been doing this for years. I felt that this was clearly a test, and I was sure it was one I was going to fail.

When they arrived at her home, I prefaced the conversation by explaining that I really wasn't a psychic and that maybe this wasn't the best idea. But they assured me that they had not come to test me but to ask me to get information to help them. They explained that sometimes, although psychics can help others, they are often too close to their own issues to see them clearly, and they wind up coloring things with their own emotions. It's kind of like when you can't see the forest for the trees. I understood that feeling.

Both of those readings went remarkably well, and all three of them said that they would like to start referring people to me. Again, I tried to explain that I wasn't a psychic, but the referrals began anyway. Soon I found myself writing Margaret's messages for several people a month. One day a reading took a different twist when Margaret helped a client to communicate with her mother, who had passed on almost a year earlier. Now it is not uncommon for people to come to me in order to speak to a loved one who has crossed over.

As time went on, I grew more confident in the readings because of Margaret's uncanny way of touching people's minds and souls—no matter what the situation.

About a year later, Margaret made a new request. She said it was time for me to create a system that would teach others to do what she and I were doing. She asked me to create a workshop that would open them up to angelic and other communication. I was to use the skills I had already developed. "Do what you do best," she said.

The resulting workshop was a combination of original music, energetic exercises, and guided imagery, which came to be known as *Angels and Shamans*. Through this workshop, hundreds of participants have received the names of their angels and have conversed with them for the first time. That was in 1994, and since that time I have continued to do what have come to be called "angel letters" while also teaching people how to communicate directly with their angelic partners.

At the end of 2010, Margaret offered a new request. She asked me compose a book of her messages that would help those who dwell on the earth to understand the true essence of their being and why this is going to be such a pivotal time in history.

I began this book in December of 2010, and it evolved over the next months as certain situations in the world evolved. It has been an incredible experience for me, because when you are channeling information, you are both writing and reading the book at the same time! When I first set out to write this book, a good friend of mine said she couldn't wait to read it, and my honest response was, "Me, too!"

All of the chapters that follow, unless otherwise noted, are messages that I received from Margaret and recorded in this book. Remember that these messages are coming from a place of *nonjudgment* and wil allow you to look at your lives with the luxury of seeing them in the light of a much *bigger picture*. As I edited the material, I realized that Margaret intended to do three things: to dispel the myths we have all learned that deny us the personal power that the truth brings us; illuminate some of the most misunderstood and greatest truths about the nature of humankind, spirit, and the Creator; and finally introduce some very specific techniques that we can use to lift ourselves—body, mind, and spirit—into the lives that will bring us the greatest joy as individuals and as a planet.

One of the things writing this book did for me—and I hope it will do it for you as well—was to bring all of the experiences of my life into clearer focus. I can see so clearly now how all of the decisions I have made have created my current life. I can see how they created my strengths and challenges. The difference is that after writing (and reading) this book, I have a sense of how powerful we all are and how close we really are to the Creator of all things. I learned that we are only one step away from the angels, they are only one step away from the infinite intelligence that created everything we know, and we are all interconnected to that source.

Now my goal is to continue to explore new ways to best tap into the limitless supply of love, energy, and wisdom that we have available at our core and to share that information with all of you.

Thank you for joining me on the journey,
Gerry

CHAPTER 2

TOUCHED BY AN ANGEL

> *I promise you that if you*
> *open your mind to the concepts*
> *within this book, it will*
> *change your life!*

Hello, dear ones, and welcome. I am an angel. I do not mean that in a figurative sense. I mean it quite literally! I have existed since before the beginning of that which you know as time and was among those that were first created when the Creator expanded himself (or herself, or itself, if you prefer) into all that we know to exist today.

Angels were created to be co-creators, to develop and separate the light and the darkness; the warm and the cold; all of the creatures that exist on the land, under the sea, and in the sky. If you were to picture the Creator as the Chief Executive Officer of Creation, then we were created as second in command. The spirit essence of the Creator splintered into millions of "middle managers" whose role it was to execute the vision of the Creator in expanding his essence into eternity.

We evolved, almost instantaneously, into our roles of protector, messenger, creator, muse, and the voice of blissful harmony.

My name is Margaret, although throughout the centuries I have been known by many other names. Since the dawn of time, I have spoken through many human voices, all of whom carried the message of peace, joy, and *nonjudgment.* In the early 1990s, I began to speak with Gerry. As he previously mentioned, he wondered what made him qualified to communicate with angels. He was not someone who was deeply ingrained in a religious community or who had some saintly spiritual qualities. He was, to the contrary, very human and filled with very typical human qualities. What led me to him was that *he called to me.* He asked for my assistance with his life, and in turn, he later asked me a question that we are not often asked: "How can I be of help to you?" Yes, Gerry had studied to develop his spiritual communication skills to be open to spiritual messengers. But it was his surrender to the concept that he was lost, and his request to know me, that led him to speak to me, and the door was opened.

"It can't be that easy," I can hear you saying. "Everyone could talk to angels if that were true." To this I say—you are right; everyone can speak to angels. The purpose of my relationship with Gerry, and the work that he has done since our meeting, is to carry out this message to others:

Everyone can speak to angels, and they can hear them as well!

This is a very crucial time in human history. Angels are attempting to reach out to the greatest number of people on the planet, and I have chosen to do so through this book as well as the *Messages from Margaret* blog, Facebook posts, and other communications that I have asked Gerry to share. These technologies are some of your most popular forms of communication. We attempt to carry these messages forth to millions upon millions of seekers who also would like to speak to their angels—the same angels that assisted with their creation and who vibrate deeply within their souls.

You already know us. You have already spoken to us many times. We are the quiet inner voice that urges you to check your gas gauge when your car is almost out of gas. We are the voice of the muse that sparks your creativity or the voice that tells you that there is more to life than that for which you have settled. We are the voice that reminds you to be grateful when you remember how much you have and the voice that brings you home when it is time to cross over. We are the quiet voice that exists within your soul.

There is a reason why this book is so very important right now; not to say that it was not important before, but in today's worldwide energy there is a pervasive energy of fear. That fear is ruining the economies of the world, which are driven by the need for an optimistic outlook on the future. You measure investments by their monetary value, but investments are, in fact, dreams. They are dreams for the future, which are based on all of the best facts that can be gleaned to support them. Pervasive fear gives way to difficulty creating positive outlook and a lack of trust in the future. But it is not only the economy that is feeling the uncertainty of fear. There is, throughout the world, an overall dissatisfaction with its leaders. The people are becoming conscious. They are rising up and asking for fairness and equity and leaders who are working for a common good.

The world has been calling out for someone, or something, to help you as you are feeling so powerless. This is not a new thing. Throughout history, angels have responded to the call for help and have appeared to every type of human, offering the same message over and over: *fear not!* We say this not because people we appear to are afraid of us; in fact, we possess an energy that most would feel as calming and reassuring. The message of *fear not* is the message in its entirety. Fear is a polarizing emotion, and it leads to inertia or decline. But it is not simply an emotion; it is a powerful overall energy.

Those who have come to *this book* have done so because you are seeking a way to make sense of where you are in your life and of the world in general.

It is designed to help you to understand three things: who you are, where you came from, and how to take positive and loving control of where you are going!

For many of you, some of the things I will say in this book will make great sense, while for others it will challenge your beliefs, and some may even find them controversial.

I promise you that if you open your mind to the concepts within this book, it will change your life! It is impossible for you to embrace the reality of who you truly are and not have it create a different energy around you, which in turn will create a powerful and more blissful reality. And at the same time as you are reading this, the worldwide energy is shifting in such a way that the timing of your changed thinking could not be more opportune.

Peace and love to all,
Margaret

CHAPTER 3

THE MYTH
OF CREATION

> *Now is the first time that there
> is the potential for a major
> portion of humankind to
> understand that they actually
> are creating this life.*

To understand where you are going and how to get there, it is necessary to first understand where you began. I will then start at the very beginning and illuminate the background story of creation, because it is the key to everything that brings us to this crucial time in history.

There are those who believe that humankind is heading toward the dawn of Armageddon, a fitting end for a society that has created munitions capable of destroying a majority of the life-forms that currently inhabit the earth.

For others, there is the belief that you are clearly validating religious prophecies of a second coming, in which the Creator will send his son to earth to judge the living and to destroy those who do not deserve to be on this planet, leaving the earth only with those who would create a world of peace and humanity.

There are those who believe that the earth, stressed to her breaking point, will unleash a torrent of natural disasters, leaving the planet redesigned into an unrecognizable form. And then there are those who believe that extraterrestrials will come to Earth to share their wisdom about systems to reduce the carbon production of the planet and save it from eventual extinction.

Why, then, have I asked Gerry to write this book when so much information, and opinion, is already there for the taking? Quite simply, it is because there is the potential for all of the above to be true . . . or for none of the above to be true . . . *and the ultimate destiny of the planet has been placed in the hands of you, my dear reader, and those with whom you have influence.*

There is no mistake or misprint. Each person who has been attracted to this book has chosen to become a key to the survival of the planet and of his or her friends and loved ones. But before you choose not to read on, frightened by the feeling of the weight that has just been placed on your shoulders, please understand one very clear thing: You are *already* involved in the decision making of the destiny of the planet. Every single person on this planet is a decision maker of his or her ultimate destiny.

What makes you a decision maker rests not in how you vote, not in your social or political awareness, and not in your actions or inaction. *You are a decision maker simply because of one thing and one thing alone: the way you think.* It was the original *thought* that caused all of creation to become reality, and that same power has been handed down to every single person on this planet. It makes you as powerful as the President of the United States or any king or leader of any country or union of countries.

Now is the first time that there is the potential for a major portion of humankind to understand that we actually are *creating* this life. When Jesus said, "This and more you will do," he was telling humankind that it was possible for miracles to be performed by all humans. He went even further in saying that the power of your consciousness gave you the power to do even more than he had demonstrated.

It is your individual thought that combines with the individual thoughts of others through a process called the Law of Magnetic Resonance, which works quite simply and is the basis of all creation.

You see, dear ones, many of you have been taught that in the beginning there was only darkness and that the Creator gave birth to the universe by first thinking of that which he desired to create and then the words, "Let there be light." This is the myth that has been presupposed for centuries, but I say to you that in the beginning there existed only thought, and that thought existed in the form of pure and omnipresent light or what I will call the origin of the *positive magnetic charge.*

This charge existed in bliss and in a state of pure consciousness but sought to expand and share its consciousness, which was the beginning of the power of conscious thought. But to expand, the Creator realized that he would have to set this energy in motion and there would be a need for a polar opposite, a negative charge that would allow for the creation of matter and antimatter—finite particles of creation that would come to be called "cells" and "atoms."

The Creator contracted its energy into a small, dense form, creating the first fusion. The resulting explosion of energy, which some have come to call the big bang, gave way to matter and antimatter, positive and negative charges, and darkness and light. All of the particles, however different, were interconnected to the Creator and a part of its essence.

There were new beings that sprang from the Creator's original thought and began the process of what has now come to be known as creation. The first of these beings were angels, and I am honored to have been among some of the earliest of our form. Some were created of the positive matter and some of the negative, some as beings of light and others that could not connect to the light. These angels contained the consciousness of the Creator and continued to create, in concert with the thoughts of the Creator, an entire universe, the perfect balance of all things light and all things dark. Positive and negative in charge, the magnetic resonance of these things allows the universe to be held in place by the pull of these polar opposites.

The creatures of the day and night were created and so existed . . . until humankind found fire and realized that its light and warmth would allow them to inhabit the night in a waking state. We are at the dawn of the end of another age of darkness, and humankind is about to discover another form of light that will change the face of the future.

All that exists is therefore interconnected to the Creator, the originator of the *thought* that gave birth to creation. Following the creation of the angels, the Creator shared with us the plan for the rest of the universe, and the angels in turn continued the process and gave birth to the next level, the spirits, that would come to inhabit all of what would follow. You are those spirits. I will hereafter refer to you as the *whole spirit, the soul,* or *the higher self.*

We are connected to each other and to the Creator by the strands of what you have come to call DNA. The angel that created you also aided in the creation of thousands upon thousands of other humans, plants, stones, and other creatures that share a common creative thread with you. Your connection to that angel is what establishes it as your protector, or *guardian angel.* You are a part of that angel's consciousness, just as you are a part of the consciousness of the Creator, and all beings share those thoughts in a universal or collective consciousness. Just as there is no snowflake that is exactly like another, there is no *whole spirit* that is exactly like another.

Part of what makes you so unique is your ability to continue to invent and reinvent yourself through your own creative thought. It is not unlike when you cook a dish or make a cake. Each individual ingredient will have its own flavor or quality or texture, but by combining them in differing quantities and combinations, we create entirely new flavors that have their own unique taste. But they all began from the same ingredients—just as did all of creation.

So if we can all accept that when we cook an egg it will taste different if we choose to add cheese or hot sauce, then it makes sense that just as we can add certain elements to our food, we equally can add certain elements to our overall life by the decisions that we make and the things that we think or dwell upon.

Most cultures will agree that the best way for a story to be told or a truth to be relayed is through one who is an *eyewitness* to that story or truth. Angels were and are the eyewitnesses of creation and all that has followed. We do not ascribe to judgment about how history or humankind has evolved. Rather, we just witness, in the true sense of the word. We are a part of you and you a part of us, and together we can partner with the Creator into an entirely new world of *creation*.

CHAPTER 4

THE MYTH OF SEPARATION

If we accept that humankind originated from a singular energy, and that this singular energy is at the core of everything, then it is logical that all of creation is, at some level, related and connected.

As we discussed in the previous chapter, everything that exists came from the same source, the Creator. These various forms of that original energy, patterned by individual angels, have evolved over many incarnations but have always remained interconnected. Every creature is linked together through that common core, but they are different in their unique originality. If it were not for this originality, there would be no unique creations. You would all desire the same things—the same food, the same music, the same god. The Creator intended to *expand* itself by bursting forth beings that would have a multitude of capabilities, and therefore the possibilities for continual creation were infinite.

But in order to constantly create new expressions of the Creator's plan, humans incarnate in many different scenarios. The various stories of your existence are what many belief systems have come to call lifetimes. To try and best understand this concept, think of the making of a movie. There is a beginning of the story, a middle, and an end. If the story is about the lifetime or struggles of a person, or group of people, it will tell the story of that span of time. Sometimes there will be sequels so we can learn more about where these characters are going, and in some cases there are prequels that tell the back story of how these characters came to be, maybe even about their family's history.

Now imagine for a moment that you have recorded your favorite story and had the prequel, the main story, and the sequels in order, and then you fast-forwarded through them. If you were to do this, you would get a slight sense of the process of creation as it explodes forth and *expands* throughout the universe. You would be viewing various interconnected stories, reflecting information from different times, which are all playing simultaneously. Also, if you look at the structure of the word *universe,* it could be considered to mean one phrase or one word or one part of a larger story. Likewise, the universe of creation is but one story with many different interconnected parts, which are all connected to the original thought that created the original word.

Every element of creation is part of the Creator's design to expand, and we refer to the passing of time as history, or better said, *his-story.* His story began first with the thought of the story, and then the thought being solidified into energy, drawing into a giant ball of light, and then exploding from itself and becoming a million little selves, the same as cells split forth when humans create life, taking form from the formless, creating new life from the infinite nothingness.

Now imagine that a form closely akin to the infinite intelligence is created and that this form is predominantly spirit. It has knowledge of its infinite nature but has a clear mission to spread forth all that the Creator had in mind with the original thought, essentially spreading the *word.* This would describe the creation of

angels, and from this first level of creation, the universe was created, and various incarnations of all creatures began to be formed.

As we watched our creations manifest and grow and act upon
each other, we refined our creations, and as the human race developed, you began to do the same, starting from your perfect spiritual form and entering into body after body in story after story of
the physical form. You learned how to navigate various forms, to
grow in thought, and to experience the full scope of the polarity
of your essence. You have been good, and you have been evil. You
have been vegetable and mineral. You have been male, and you
have been female, with all of this happening in what you might
sense now as the blink of an eye.

The essence of your energy, your spirit self, or what some have
come to call your *higher self,* exists apart from, but connected to,
all of your human forms and can see you at all times in all of your
stories, which is the word I will use moving forward in this chapter
rather than the words *incarnations* or *lifetimes.* I do this because
your lives are essentially your own *creative story,* which then becomes a part of the great anthology known as *his-story,* or again,
what you better know as history.

This is really what comprises time if one were to actually have
a way to measure it. A life takes place not in the measurement of
sunups and sundowns but of your life story. Your lives are lived
and reflected upon, and the sequels to the stories are lived and
reflected upon, as well as the prequels, and all are examined in
order to have a better understanding of the big story. And in the
collective consciousness, those stories are shared with each other
so that all can experience the vast richness of life.

Do you see how even the human art of storytelling, which all
of your cultures have developed, is so clearly like your spiritual
nature? All of your cultures have handed down legends, fables,
parables, and mythologies that, because you came from the same
source, have contained many great similarities.

The psychologist Carl Jung tapped into this concept in his
theories of behavioral analysis and referred to it as the *collective
unconscious.* He described the collective experiences that would

unknowingly affect a person's motivations and decision making as his or her *personal unconscious,* and those experiences that would affect the thought patterns of humankind in general as the *collective unconscious.* He coined it the "unconscious mind" because the person was not aware that these patterns of thought were affecting his or her behavior. From a larger viewpoint, however, I would say that it is the rational thinking of the physical man that is actually the unconscious, because it is not aware of the larger picture that the conscious spiritual self sees. It is interesting to note that you have created the word *conscience,* which essentially means to distinguish between good and evil. However, if you really look at the word, it can be divided into two: *con,* which means "to go against," and *science,* which comes from the Latin word meaning "knowledge." Therefore, conscience could be interpreted to mean "going against that which you rationally know and understand." That definition makes sense if you look at humankind as working within an unconscious state in which consciousness is only achieved when you tap into a *greater* perspective.

If we accept that humankind originated from a singular energy, and that this singular energy is at the core of everything, then it is logical that all of creation is, at some level, related and connected. Regardless of race, geographic location, or religious belief system, you are all created from the same original substance as the angelic kingdom and all living things. As we helped the Creator to bring the thought of the universe into reality, so too are you doing the same, and we are assisting you in this work when we are called upon.

This theory of the connectedness of humankind is not a new one. It is one that has been spoken for centuries, and it is one that has been at the core of many teachings from many prophets. Why then is it one that is so hard for humankind to accept? Why do humans seem to have a need to feel that they are better than another person, that their religion is better than that of another person, or that their race is better than that of another person? The answer is really far simpler than you would imagine.

Every creature has a need, at some level, to feel a sense of connection to its Creator. The essence of the Creator is that of a being of pure love, and many who have gone through near-death experiences have returned with the story of entering the light and feeling a sense of warmth and love like they have never known. Humans recall that state in the deepest of their untouched memories. But you become removed from it when you take a physical form and then further removed from it when you leave the body of a human mother. This sets into motion a sense of separation, which will lead you to seek out many different ways of hopefully reclaiming that feeling of connection. You will sometimes feel it in friendships, or family. You will sometimes find it in a sexual relationship; you will sometimes feel it in the fellowship and tradition of a church; and others will sometimes find it in the stillness of meditation and other spiritual practices.

What you are longing to feel is a sense of belonging, of total and unconditional acceptance, unconditional love, and total completion and security.

But most of the time you do not feel this connection, and somewhere deep inside you continue to seek it out in your work or your relationships or your religions; some even find it through drugs, alcohol, or other addictions. You may not be aware that you are seeking this, but when you find some semblance of it, you want to hold on to it and worry that maybe there will not be enough of it to go around. Because you see with human eyes and not the heart, which is more closely connected to the *essence* of spirit, you see yourselves as being different from other people, and you cannot understand how the Creator could love that other one if he or she is so different from you. You want to feel special. You want the Creator to see you and your family and your friends as special.

I have come here to dispel this myth of separation—to dispel the concept you have created that says that any one person, group, or religion is any greater in the eyes of the Creator. This is not truth. The belief that you are in some way better than another person actually comes from a need to feel personally entitled to the love of the Creator. It is the desire to feel special. You may even look to follow historical texts that show your race, or your way of thought, as somehow more preferable to the Creator. Some call their book the Bible, others call it the Koran, and still others the Covenant, the Book of Mormon, and so on. This is not unlike how a child will vie for the attention and love of a mother or father by trying to expose another sibling when he or she has done something that is bad or "breaking the rules." In that way, the child is alerting the parent that the other child is less deserving of the mom or dad's love than the "good child" is. When you are judging another, you are essentially displaying exactly the same behavior—trying to instill in yourself the feeling of being the "good child" or the "right child."

I have come today to tell you, in a very classic, angelic fashion, to fear not. The love of the Creator goes out to all of you because you are all a part of the Creator, and it is a part of all of you. No one religion is right, and no one religion is wrong. They are all expressions of a desire to reconnect with the divine. No one race is the preferred race. These are only *thoughts* that you have created to make yourselves feel right. By feeling that you have the right to judge another, you move yourself farther away from the *essence* of your being, even though when you do so you feel more "right" about yourself. That is why other prophets and Jesus said, "Judge not lest ye be judged." He was not speaking of the judgment of the Creator, but rather of the energy that you bring to yourself when you judge—because when you judge another, you reinforce the belief that you are of a higher value in the eyes of the Creator, which negates the fact that the Creator is within all of you, not outside, and you then separate yourself even more. "Whatever you do to the least of my creations you do to me" referred to humans assigning a value to creation and therefore assigning a value to themselves in relationship to the Creator. Understand that just because something was created in a certain order, or hierarchy, does not mean that one thing is any less, or more, important to the whole of creation. If you build a car, one of the last things to go into it is the battery, but the car will not operate without it.

There is no one grain of sand on a beach that is any more important than the other. No droplet of rain that provides water for you to drink is looked upon with more importance than another. It all comes from the Creator as a part of the great balance, the great harmony, and the unity of all things.

The sharps and the flats of the musical scale, when combined with the primary notes, create beautiful melodies and "c(h)ords." I use this spelling because the "h" is silent, and in fact, not only is it silent but it is truly unnecessary for the word. Chords in music are like cords that hold other things together. They are fibers of sound that connect the individual notes to the other, allowing them to portray in music that which is true of all in life. Each person vibrates with its own frequency and its own tone, but together each individual note creates collective songs and great compositions and symphonies.

We are all individual instruments that play our own individual melody as a part of the whole orchestration, just as our individual stories are all a part of history. Sometimes the song is beautiful and soft and melodic, and sometimes it is dark and foreboding, but it is all a part of the ongoing beauty of creation.

We all create. We all orchestrate. We all are players, and in the words of the great seer William Shakespeare, "All the world's a stage."

To think that anything that exists is separate of the other is a myth, and it is time for myths to be broken.

CHAPTER 5

THE MYTH OF TIME

> *. . . you are living in a place*
> *where there is a miniscule*
> *space between the past, and the*
> *present, and the future, and by*
> *reading the words on this page,*
> *you have experienced the past,*
> *present, and future all in the*
> *space of a breath.*

You all are aware of the controversy that the year 2012 experienced because of one thing in particular: the Mayan Calendar. It was a popular conception that this calendar, which only marked time up until the final month of the year 2012, indicated that this was therefore the end of life as we know it. I had always spoken to the fact that this was not the case and that these fears were unfounded, and early in 2012 archeologists discovered more writings that indicated a continuation of that calendar. But even if this had not been discovered, how accurate is the marking of time?

The calendar evolved to mark patterns of solar and other planetary activity, and it was refined to adjust to inexplicable changes in the patterns of the seasons that would reoccur after a certain number of years. It is humorous to me how powerful calendars have become. Humankind has become so accepting of it that you created rhymes about "30 days has September, April, June, and November" but all other months have 31 days, except for the odd month of February, which has 28, except when it sometimes has 29. As arbitrary as this all sounds, you all accept this as an exact science!

It is just so interesting to me the things that humankind has come to call science.

But what is more interesting about calendars is that humankind is the only creature on the planet that uses them. Every other creature lives one moment and one sunup to nightfall at a time, honoring the passing of each and settling into a pattern of behavior that feels best to their bodies for that existence. Only humankind marks the highlights of their lives by the passing of a certain number of boxes on a piece of paper that in essence does the same thing: it marks the passing of the light and the darkness, the perfect balance of that which was designed at creation. Time has been dissected into the smallest intervals possible, and I share with you that the roots of this marking of time began as a way to understand and control two things: to know how to plan for growing crops and to try to project how long a society would last. Nowadays, calendars are used more for convenience, planning, and marking important milestones—either personal or ones that mark crucial moments in the world's development as human beings.

But there are things that defy the comfortable definition of time. As you read this, you are moving from the present to the past, literally in the movement of your eye. The words you just read are in the past . . . and now these words are in the past . . . and see . . . it just happened again . . . words in the past! Can you see what a fine line the present is from the past? It is measured in nanoseconds, and as such, it means that you are living in a place where there is a miniscule space between the past, the present, and the future, and by reading the words on this page, you have experienced the past, present, and future all in the space of a breath.

Another example of the bending of time exists in the ability to speak to another person at the other end of the planet in another time zone. You are speaking on the phone from New York to California to someone who is living in the past, and you are in the future, so to speak. Or when speaking to someone on another continent, you may actually be speaking to someone who is a full day ahead or behind your time—and yet you are speaking to him or her in what you have come to call real time. Think on this for a moment. When you look through a telescope through to deep space, you are seeing images that are literally light-years away. I love that term because it is so accurate. The Creator, the being of light, has created such a vast universe that it is light-years apart, in the past or the future. If you are looking through a telescope today, those images you see are now well in the past. To your physical eyes they are happening right here and now, yet you are witnessing that image of creation or destruction as it took place ages ago.

The measurement of time is really very fluid. We could be well into the 2600s or more if time had not been broken into B.C. and A.D. Time was created to help give you a way to measure, just like a yardstick or measuring cup. It is a way for you to attempt to re-create with some regularity, so that you can have more control over what often seemed to be a random creative process.

So why, if time is then somewhat illusory, is it so important to create long-standing calendars? Why throughout history have people studied the stars and the movement of the sun? What were they looking to learn? Essentially they learned that certain astrological phenomena created patterns. They watched how children born in specific cycles of the earth, in various growing, reaping, and tilling seasons, had certain behavioral characteristics. They learned that place and time of when a life occurs in the astrological formation of the stars and planets was important to the makeup and characteristics of that person. They noticed what Jung would later call the collective behaviors of adults born in different cycles and saw that entire generations would repeat certain behaviors. Some would be more war loving and some

31

more peace loving. Some would be more creative and artistic while others would work harder and produce more crops or housing. Based on these things, they began to develop a calendar that portrayed how the descendants of that generation would likely fare—and how the growing trends of the food sources of the earth were also affected by these stellar cycles. They also saw that every certain number of years there were quantum leaps in the knowledge that the people would acquire. Again, this was based on both the history of behaviors they could see repeated and the traits they could see forthcoming. The first creators of calendars were a combination of what you would call astronomers and astrologists. And they attempted to create a system that would help to predict how humans interacted with the natural order. To do this they tried to apply some type of mathematical way to chart the progression of sunups to sundowns, and the first calendars were born. I would actually refer to these early time recorders as astro-numerologists.

There is often a great deal of truth that can be seen in charting the astrological aspects of a person's behavior. Let us look first at that word as the basis for the science: *astro,* referring to the astro-magnetic push or pull that is exerted at a particular point in time, such as the time of birth, and *logical,* that which can be predicted to a certain degree of accuracy based on the study of particular variables.

Many ancient scholars were very adept at the astrological interpretation of history and as such, were equally capable of a somewhat clear projection of the future. There is, of course, no adequate way to totally predict the future because every being is imbued with the characteristic of free will. It is this free will that will allow you to make decisions at any given moment that will totally change the focus of your future and the future of others, and often those decisions cannot be easily predicted.

So if we can accept that humankind can now, on a daily basis, utilize technology that essentially bends the parameters of time, and that because of your capability to make decisions based on free will it is difficult, if not impossible, to always accurately predict human activity, then I would pose the theory that time and the creation of measurements of time are basically flawed. They are therefore a myth that holds you to another concept of your own limitations. It further places you in the position of focusing on past times or future times to the extent that many forget the only place that holds all of your energetic power—the present time. So now, just as humankind has created time, it is time for humankind to allow itself to accept that it can expand its concepts.

CHAPTER 6

THE PERFECT STORM

You, humankind, have created the perfect storm of knowledge, accessibility to communication, the financial dependence of those in power on the masses, and a new generation that has grown up not knowing a time without these tools. Substantial change and shifting of power back to the people at large are therefore unavoidable.

So let's see where we have come thus far. We spoke in an earlier chapter about the essence of creation and how humankind is just as much a part of the creative expansion as are angels and the Creator. We further spoke about how placing your thoughts in the past or the future is actually based on limited theories of time, constructed from calendars that have no real scientific validity. And further expanding the concept of time, we also discussed the myth of separation, which indicated that every incarnation in every period of history is all going on at one time and is part of the larger anthology as inspired by the original story written by the Creator and interpreted by you individual authors known as humankind.

How you are reacting to this information may depend very much on your current beliefs and perceptions. As humans are the authors of their own stories, and since there are billions of stories being played out on just this planet, then clearly there are a myriad of interpretations that are being put forward. Many will take shape according to the consciousness of the author and whether he or she is a "glass half-full" or "glass half-empty" type of person.

Those who see life as a glass half-empty subscribe to doom-and-gloom theories and believe that, if we look at what is happening around us—wars, economic distress, natural disasters on the increase, environmental conditions on the decline, and the ongoing struggle of our own lives—they are clear indicators that the world is in a bad way. To them it is very likely that the world is headed toward some type of cataclysmic ending.

To the "glass half-full" group, the world is changing for the better. People are wasting less and saving more. They see the growth of an overall environmental consciousness, not among just governments but people in general. They see how Internet communities, such as Facebook and Twitter, have connected the planet and fostered the ability for groups of freedom-loving unknowns to actually be the seed of the overturning of governments. They see this as just the beginning!

But there is a third group as well. This is the group that is very rarely spoken about. They see the glass as just a glass with water in it, and their only question is not if the glass is half-full or half-empty, but rather is it bottled or tap water? This is the largest group in the world at this time. They are people who live life in a day-to-day vacuum of logical self-interest, with little care or regard for their effect on the future. They are using all of their focus just to get by—week to week, day to day, and paycheck to paycheck. This is the disenfranchised majority who has grown weary of politics and no longer believes in government or religious organizations.

They could not care less about the accuracy of calendars and feel badly about the natural disasters they hear of on the news but are happy these things didn't happen to them. Many would love to do something different with their lives, but they feel stuck in what and where they are. They want to see the glass as half-full, but they have been disappointed so many times by the half-full glass just evaporating before their eyes that they would rather not think about the glass at all.

I would venture to say that, even if you identify yourself as a half-full or half-empty person, that when I described this last group, you could identify with it as well, and that is a good thing! It means that you have embraced your life as a human being, that you have owned the fact that you came here in a human body, and that, first and foremost, you are honoring your human concerns. It says that although you have drunk from half-empty and half-full glasses, you are still willing to go back to drink again. You, dear ones, are what will be the deciding factor in the determination of what the future will actually mean to humankind.

You are the group that will determine the mind-set of your households, your neighborhoods, your countries, and finally your planet! The power of your creative consciousness is so strong that, if harnessed correctly, you can restructure disappointment to appointment. *Appointment* has two meanings in your culture. First, it refers to being placed into a position by a person or group that is a higher authority. The second meaning is to set aside a time in your day to complete a specific task. Conversely, *disappointment* refers to the sadness or regret that occurs when something that was hoped for or expected does not come to fruition.

In the process of creation, you have been *appointed* by the Creator to use your inherent abilities to expand creation. To do this, you made tools to help you set goals and measure the success of your actions. One of those tools that you have created is time. The measurement of time allows you to task your overall appointment by the Creator into smaller appointments to do certain tasks that have a specific purpose. You make an appointment to see the dentist as part of the larger appointment to care for the body that you inhabit. You choose to attend a fund-raiser in order to help those in greater need.

Disappointment comes in when you realize that appointments have not been met, when promises are not kept, and when you can feel deep down inside, *This isn't how things were meant to be.*

It is this feeling of deep disappointment in the leaders you have appointed to help you realize your goals that has led to the lack of trust that most people now feel in governments, churches, financial institutions, businesses, and sometimes even yourselves and each other.

But trust in yourself, and your brother's creative ability, is exactly what is most needed at this time. You can turn trust into manifestation, you can turn frustration into creation, and finally you can turn the glass half-full and the glass half-empty into the glass that is overflowing constantly. This and more are all within your reach and all within your power. It is your birthright—because it existed in you prior to this birth and still exists within you! You need only to tap into it to allow it to come to the surface.

Whether you call yourself Baby Boomers, Generation X, Generation Y, yuppies, hippies, the 99 percent, or the 1 percent—whatever group you identify with—you have all decided to be born into and to share this one time in history. It is the time of change. Change is the only constant in the universe. You are always changing. There are no two days that are exactly alike. You are aging, you are learning new things, and you are growing. There are those of you who may have seen the original *Star Trek* TV series. The crew spoke into wireless communicators that at the time of the show's creation were clearly science fiction. Today, almost all of you communicate with cell phones without even a thought as to how they work or how this science fiction has now become reality. All of what now exists began as just a thought, first from the Creator, then from the angels, and then from humankind. You are the ongoing creators and authors of all that is fiction and nonfiction. All thought begins as fiction. It all begins as something outside of the realm of reality. But thought then draws to it the like energy that assists it in becoming reality. Like energy attracts like energy.

I would ask you to take a moment and think about how many things have changed in the course of just your lifetime. Think about when you were little, as far back as you can remember, and what you had and did back in those days and how they differ from now.

Gerry did this and thought about the first TV that he used to watch, which had a very small screen, was black and white, and took a several minutes to warm up. Once the TV was working, there were only seven channels. The reception was completely controlled by the rabbit-ear antenna that sat above the TV, and it would be maneuvered every which way to get a good picture, with as little "snow" as possible.

Gerry's family phone had a thick cord and was a heavy black thing with a round dial. Back in his younger days, there were so few phone lines that Gerry's family shared a party line with another family, and often when they wanted to use the phone, the other family would be talking, and they would have to wait to make their call. It did, however, make for some wonderful eavesdropping!

Everything changes, and in the past 100 years, things have changed in quantum measures. Over the course of the years to come, they will change even faster. Throughout the history of this planet, humankind has taken huge leaps in the understanding of the things that they were capable of doing. Remember that it was only in the past 150 years that such inventions as the light bulb and electricity came into widespread use.

Changes in the years to come, and especially in the immediate future, will be fueled by technology, and that very technology is bringing the world closer together and into a global community. It is a new jumping-off period, and when you look at history, you can see that the growth of your planet has occurred in some very specific jumps.

You went from the individual hunter-gatherer to a more evolved agrarian society in which some people lived in the collectives of a village and later cities or towns.

When the industrial age came, there was another major leap of knowledge, and humankind developed the ability to manufacture products at a much greater capacity to take care of people over much larger geographic areas.

You developed transportation systems to carry those products, from horse-driven carriages to boats, trains, and finally planes. Think about how once only explorers could travel throughout the world; now anyone who can afford it is capable of world travel.

Inventions like the printing press allowed news to travel and knowledge to be shared among more people because of the ease in reproducing the printed word.

Then you moved into the electronic age and the invention of the radio, moving pictures, and finally television, which allowed people to both be entertained and to communicate with those on the other side of the world. Again, the world was becoming smaller, but the power to use these new tools was always in the hands of the wealthy and powerful.

Fast-forward to today, and times are beginning to change. He who controls communication controls power, and it has become increasingly obvious over the past years that the Internet—and in particular, Facebook, Twitter, and YouTube—has not only become a way for people to talk about what they are doing that evening, it has also become the platform for deep-seated social change and major governmental power shifts. Technology is moving so quickly that it is very possible that by the time you read this book, there will be newer and more exciting communication tools, which will unite the planet even more.

You have navigated from the agrarian age to the industrial age to the information age, and we are about to enter another age—*the age of consciousness!* You may recall that we spoke briefly about the essence of consciousness. Consciousness is that space where your mind connects with the *essence* of the Creator, and in so doing, the individual develops the ability to transcend logic, which can sometimes limit the creative nature. It is the place that sees not what is, but rather what can be.

The current shift is allowing the individual to become powerful beyond the limitations that he or she and society have set. It is a completely new playing field that expands global knowledge, new friendships, and an enhanced sense of self-responsibility. Humans are moving toward a simpler time that will both encourage and assist individuals to require less of governments and more of themselves. This, coupled with even more substantial social networks, will allow humankind to truly have the potential to become a united planet. And the best part is that the very corporations that are supporting the growth of all of these worldwide communication devices are actually making themselves financially dependent on the individual, so any action to restrict their growth will not occur because it is not in the financial interest of these companies.

You, humankind, have created the perfect storm of knowledge, accessibility to communication, the financial dependence of those in power on the masses, and a new generation that has grown up not knowing a time without these tools. Substantial change and shifting of power back to the people at large are therefore unavoidable.

Which is what makes this so very exciting. In their desire to create a worldwide system of communication that has as its basis the increase of profits, the large corporations have actually created a worldwide community. That worldwide community is helping to dispel the myth of separation, and they are dispelling the myth of time by constant contact with followers and friends and likes in every time zone—from today, tomorrow, and yesterday.

But the most powerful part of the current forms of communication, and their role in dispelling the myth of separation, is that the majority of information, knowledge, and *creativity*—which are so easily accessed—are *shared!*

Humankind is sharing with each other its passions, its anger, its beauty, and of course, its favorite funny pictures of cute kittens! You are building a worldwide community of change that begins with a single word—*share!*

CHAPTER 7

THE PARABLE OF THE KING AND "THE MATTER"

> *You need only to believe that you are bigger than the matter you see in the mirror, and you need not put all of your faith in the scientists, philosophers, or religious leaders if your heart does not resonate with their message . . .*

For years humankind has been searching for answers about its own existence. Where did you come from? Where are you going? Is there anything that exists beyond this life? And from this thought process, three disciplines have developed: science, philosophy, and religion.

The discipline of science, and with it mathematics and physics, tries to determine that there is a definitive order to the universe and that this order would prove that everything has a formula.

Formula is an interesting word to me, for it implies that everything that has a form, or matter, and therefore has some quantifiable measurement that would allow the human mind to make it more easily understood and then potentially tameable. Science can be an amazing thing, and it has evolved to the point that new "realities" are created every day. The amazing strides in cellular communication, robotic surgery, and the study of your origins in space have been fascinating and wonderful.

In truth, there *is* a perfect order to everything that exists in the universe, and there is a perfect mathematical logic to its form. But part of the mystery of science is that this form is fluid, always changing, and still being created. There are even those in the field of noetic science who have proven that the cellular structure of a substance can be changed by scientists infusing it with thought. For example, it was shown that you can change the microscopic structure of water by covering it with words that are either upsetting to the human mind or comforting and peaceful. Containers of water covered with those words were then frozen, and the water covered in loving words developed beautiful crystals. Conversely, the water covered in fearful and hateful words created ugly formations of crystals. This is part of the wonder and miracle of creation that escapes *conventional* logic.

For many scientists, their work is done in a vacuum—a church-and-state type of separation from religion. For many religious leaders, science is considered the enemy of faith because it defies the traditional writings in the holy books by trying to offer logical explanations for things that are taught to be above the comprehension of the mortal man.

Philosophy binds the two worlds together because it longs to create rational thought processes around complicated esoteric concepts such as "I think, therefore I am." Philosophy seeks to explain the human condition, the relationship between man and god, and the essence of the voice inside your head that has come to be referred to as thought. Today there are even religions that approach their beliefs through a combination of science and philosophy and with a smattering of faith in the unknown.

For centuries, the three factions have fought each other—or should I say, debated each other—as to what method of thinking is the most valid. Different cultures look differently on which is the right thinking, and many embrace a combination of the disciplines' independent thoughts.

I come today to tell you that all three disciplines have the potential to be correct or incorrect. All three are a part of the greater truth. As stories are often the best form of communicating a complex concept, I would like to offer the following story:

What Is the Matter?

A long, long time ago there was a very wise king who was beloved by his people. He was so loved because he had created a kingdom that respected and protected the individual thoughts of his subjects. Here you would find scientists and philosophers and different practitioners of religious belief systems and occult practices. The king's allowance of varied thought was not totally without self-service. He was of the mind that if he were to be all-powerful, then it was necessary for him to be aware of all the ways that power could be derived, and so he and his most trusted advisors would learn from all those who practiced many ways of thinking and believing.

One day, while taking a walk on the grounds of his palace, the king came across a golden puddle of liquid, which was pooled at the bottom of a cypress tree. He touched the liquid, which was both cold and then warm and became solid when droplets touched his fingers. When he blew on it, the pool reshaped and then would return to its original form but grew larger with each breath blown. The king summoned his scientists, who examined it and determined that the liquid had to be some form of gold that had dissolved and was unable to harden again. But when they tried to scoop it up into a bowl, no matter how much they scooped, the original amount remained. After filling

45

60 vessels with the gold substance, they were baffled and determined that there must be an underground spring of the substance. But they could not find the source.

Growing impatient, the king summoned his religious leaders. Some viewed it as a spell that had been cast by an enemy that would produce a gold that could not be used or formed. Others considered it a blessing and a sign from the gods that the king was revered by the gods, because he had found the substance. Still others believed that the king should pour the liquid into a mold to create a crown, since clearly this was a very powerful substance and for him to mold it into something that was a symbol of his position would show the power of the king and how he was revered by the gods. Others felt that a great sacrifice should be prepared to the gods to thank them for having bestowed this new substance, and still others believed that this was creating false idols and that the substance should be buried and ignored as temptation.

He listened and then called for his great thinkers, his philosophers, to dwell on the meaning of the matter and what it might be. Some dwelled on whether the matter really existed at all—or was all of this just a dream to begin with? Others admitted that the matter existed but that its ability to re-create itself, to take different forms and still be the same, meant that this substance may be the essence of the original substance that the king, because of his wise nature, had discovered while others had missed it. But they too were unable to come up with a clear concept of what the substance was. They agreed that if it had form and was visible to each of them then it existed. They were able to see it, feel it, smell it, and even taste it.

The king thought long and hard on all of the theories and then went out that evening to sit by the cypress tree and think some more. But when he arrived at the tree, the golden liquid was gone and the leaves of the tree had taken on the same golden hue and were falling to the ground. He wondered at first if the liquid had been stolen and called his guards, but just then, his scientists came to him to say that the liquid in the vessels had disappeared as well, right in front of their eyes—gone from a form to nothing.

The king went back to his chambers to try to make sense of this. He pondered these thoughts:

- There was a matter that I could see today and never saw before.

- It could change from soft and flowing to hard, depending on what touched it.

- When new breath was breathed into it, it would grow larger.

- Even though it was placed in containers, it still remained in its original form at the source.

- It then just vanished, just as it appeared. Where had it gone and where it came from was a total mystery.

He thought and thought and finally fell into a deep sleep and began to dream.

In his dream, he was flying on the back of a great bird who took him to the top of a very high mountain. Once there, he found a beautiful golden palace, and within he saw a man who was meditating near a cypress tree. The man was resplendent and almost seemed to be transparent at the same time. When the king approached him, he was shocked to see that the man looked just like him.

"So," the man said, "you have come here to seek me out for answers to your questions?"

"I am not sure," the king answered. "Who are you, and why do you look like me?"

The transparent man laughed and said, "No, it is you who looks like me!" Had he not been in this other man's palace, the king would have been indignant at someone clearly impersonating him—but he allowed him to speak on.

"You have come here, in the dream time, to find the answer to the question of your new find. You are wondering about the nature of the matter."

"Yes, please, do you know of its origin?" said the king.

The man smiled and said, "Its origin is from the origin of all things. It comes from the source and is transmuted into the shape that will best expand the consciousness of he who views it. It appears at a given point in time and lives out its life, and although it can be reshaped, it never loses its original essence. In fact, when others breathe life into it, it actually increases its form and becomes more than it was when it originated. And finally," he said, "it will one day return to the place of its origin and vanish just as easily as it appeared."

Although the explanation was too complicated for the king's mind to comprehend, he felt his heart processing the information, and his eyes filled with tears at the realization that somewhere deep within him there was a memory of a time when he understood this and all things.

"You now understand why you were given this vision today," the man said. "The matter appeared to you as gold because it took a form that all would be able to see as a thing of value. Your scientists tried to find a way to establish the root of its production so its value could be replicated and controlled. Your religious leaders tried to assign a meaning to the substance that could allow you to re-create the matter into power and somehow use it to say that you had a closer relationship to the gods than others. And finally, the thinkers, when they could not decide what the matter was, decided that, when it vanished, it perhaps never existed at all. Or that you, because of your great intellect, had discovered something that lesser thinkers never noticed, again setting you above all others."

"And when the matter vanished," the king said, "I began to doubt that I had even seen it in the first place. I wondered what I had done wrong that I had been given this gift and then had it taken away, as though I was being punished. How would I explain this to my people and not have them doubt that it was right that I rule them? If I am fallible, then I do not deserve to rule!"

The man looked at the king and said, "When your mother and father shared their love together, they breathed life into a new form that was you, and you came into a physical existence, although you did not exist before that moment. Throughout the years, many tried to shape you into one that would be most valuable for them, and often you would take those forms, but still you remained you. And when the time came that your mother and father died, in both cases you stood by their bed and wondered where they had gone. They were there, and then, just as the breath of life formed them, the breath of life left them, and they were gone. But always, their matter, from the essence it came from, still exists. And no matter what form the matter takes, whether golden or the dirt below it, it is of equal value. *All matter is equal!*

"I," the man said, "am you. We are one. I am the essence of your creation, and I exist no matter what form you take. I will continue to exist and inspire you and will answer your internal questions when you desire to grow beyond that which you know. You need only to believe that you are bigger than the matter you see in the mirror, and you need not put all of your faith in the scientists, philosophers, or religious leaders if your heart does not resonate with their message, for they are often right and they are often wrong. That is fine."

The king then woke and, remembering his dream, called forth his scientists and religious leaders and philosophers and said that he had come to realize that *since the matter had come from the nothingness, and since the nothingness was unknown, therefore, he would decree that no one should fear the unknown, because <u>nothing was the matter.</u> And since all matter came from the source, then all things* *were to be treated as equal!* He decreed that all people in his kingdom would henceforth be allowed to fully participate in their vision of what their own personal matter was to be. All of his subjects, from that moment on, were to be treated as his equal.

"But how will we control the flow of wealth and riches and power if all people are equal?" asked his advisors. "If you are no greater than a servant, then those who are of service would be viewed with the same regard as the king!"

At that statement the king smiled and said, "And if so . . . *what would the matter be?*"

You may recall that in the previous chapters I alerted you to the truth that you are a very powerful being. As we begin to explore this new truth of recognizing that you, who are reading this book, are as powerful as any president or king, then you are coming to look at the truth that your being, your essence, and your thoughts are all a part of the same creative energy that made all things. The "matter" in the parable is symbolic of the *soul* of all matter that has been created. At the thought of the Creator, it appeared, and then through the breath of life that is given to matter by its co-creators, whether angelic or human, the matter takes new and different forms.

The thoughts of the co-creators will determine how the matter will be shaped. It can be made into something that will help expand the source of all things or that which will constrict the flow by attempting to contain it. The man the king encountered in the dream was his essence, his soul, his higher self—that spiritual form that I explained in a previous chapter who watches over the simultaneous stories that you all have created.

Finally, we finished the parable with the king coming to the realization, "Nothing is the matter." When you come from a place of fearing that you will lose your power if others have differing thoughts, looks, or levels of wealth than you, then your thoughts are driven from your perception of matter. When you come to realize that all matter comes from the same source—and that this source was a being of infinite love—then you will allow for the flow of that love, which is at the essence of all things that the Creator has devised. Then all things will have that love breathed into them and will continue to expand in love, far beyond the size of their original containers. And you will live without the thought of fear of lack or loss of personal power.

Form comes from thought. If you can keep track of where your thoughts are coming from, then you will be able to have a better idea of what experiences you are forming for yourself. If you are coming from a place of fear or hate or competition, then you are going to bring to yourself experiences that are formed around the desire to experience those thoughts.

It is not about karma. Rather, when you think of something and empower it with an emotion, then you are activating the Law of Magnetic Resonance to draw that experience to yourself. Hard as that might be to understand, this is how it happens. You are not only what you eat; you are what you think! Your soul seeks to understand every aspect of the human condition because it is then able to see how love can cure or heal that condition and how the original essence of the Creator can be restored in an even greater capacity. Everything in the universe seeks to be expanded in some form.

CHAPTER 8

EMBRACING YOUR INNER TRUTH

The truth about truth is that you already know it! You were created understanding the essence of your being, your creators, the original Creator, and all that you have created in response. But as you, over time, have placed your energy into life forms with greater density, you have lost some of your clarity.

There are times, I know, when all of you have experienced what has come to be known as the "Aha!" moment. It is that instant in time where you grasp a concept that before was alien to you. Or sometimes it is that moment when you realize that life is bigger than you had imagined it, and it changes the whole momentum of life.

For many people, those "Aha!" moments occur when they are reading something, watching a movie, or having a deep conversation in which someone explains something in just such a way that it finally hits home. It hits the true home, the place where the essence of who you are resides, and for that moment, you are connected with the consciousness of your higher self or true self, and that special feeling occurs when your brain, body, and soul are in alignment. There are other phrases that you use to describe this experience:

- That really hit me where I live.
- That brought it all home for me.
- I didn't see that coming.
- It hit me out of the blue.
- That struck me to the core.

It is, along with déjà vu, one of the only spiritually connective experiences that almost all humans experience, and as such, it links you together in a common bond worldwide. It also is the key to this chapter.

The truth about truth is that you already know it! You were created understanding the essence of your being, your creators, the original Creator, and all that you created in response. But as you, over time, have placed your energy into life-forms with greater density, you have lost some of your clarity.

Think of this logically. Let's say that you make a pitcher of iced tea, and it is originally placed in a crystal clear container. The iced tea appears to be the same in color, and you can still see the essence of the iced tea. Now let's picture that you pour it into a heavy blue glass, a frosted glass, and a plastic cup that is completely opaque. If you look at the glasses from the side, they will all contain the same liquid, but it will be hard to tell what is within them.

If you go up to the top of the glasses and look in, then you will see that regardless of the containers, they all have the same stuff within. Looking at it from an angle that is above the conventional viewpoint is what creates the "Aha!" moment.

When you remember that regardless of the form that you currently inhabit—male, female, black, white, Asian, Hispanic— or what traditional cover-up you wear, be it a shawl, a sari, a turban, a yarmulke, or a suit, underneath it there is the same original "iced tea"!

That is the essence of truth. When as humans you seek a path of truth, what you are really looking for is to simply find the "Aha!" moments. You are trying to learn how to position your thinking, your relationships, your work, and your life in such a way that you can see into the top of the glass and always be aware of your place in the whole.

This is why in a previous chapter I said that it really didn't matter if you saw the glass as half-full or half-empty, because if you are seeking the truth, then eventually you come to only see that what is filling all the glasses is the same wonderful drink. Some may, through their belief systems and heritage, see the drink as water and some as tea and some as wine and some as beer and some as malta; the list goes on and on.

But the bottom line is that we are all made of the same matter. We are all the same air and gasses and liquids and solids; all that differs is the shade and density of the container.

Is this perhaps why, when someone does not understand something, you refer to that person as "dense" or not the "brightest bulb"? It is because of the denseness of the physical cellular forms that you have taken that you are often unable to connect to the light and therefore are too dense to understand or to reflect the light in the brightest way!

This is something that has been changing over time. The physical form has been becoming smaller over time as the need for every person to perform physical work to ensure his or her survival has lessened. Most people work in careers that require far more mental activity than physical activity, and this has enabled a lessening as well in the density of the physical mind-body-spirit connection. This has also led to more of an equalization of labor being performed by men and women, thus allowing women to be a greater part of the worldwide creative process and allowing many men to open up to the more intuitive abilities that are learned through raising children.

As this has been occurring, spirits who have come into male forms and female forms have come to better understand what it means to be taking on the other's traditional roles. And as this truth begins to bring about different ways of positioning your thinking, it is allowing all of you to jockey about a bit to try to get a better view of the top of the glass. It is allowing for more universal acceptance of underlying truths of parenthood and community. The uncertain economy has also created many more extended families that are returning to the truths that were already understood by many tribal people. Many children are being raised by grandparents, and new types of families of choice have been changing to keep pace with a world that is changing faster and faster. As the worldwide community is expanding, many family units find themselves returning to the classic extended family as well.

There is great truth to be learned from the counsel of elders, and even more that can be learned through the mouths of babes. The time has come to open your minds to the wisdom of old, young, and everyone in between, for within their truth you may find the essence of yours. The time has come for all of you to remember and embrace your inner truth.

CHAPTER 9

HUMAN SEXUALITY & THE SOUL

> *There are many who*
> *truly believe that the greatest*
> *erogenous zone is the brain, but*
> *rather it is the soul itself.*

Imagine, for just a moment, that your soul or spirit is without sexual organs but is capable of sexual energy and expression far beyond anything you could currently comprehend. This is the essence of what your sexual energy is really like. There are many who truly believe that the greatest erogenous zone is the brain, but rather it is the soul itself. All of the most profound perceptions and experiences you have as a human originate in your spirit form.

Now imagine for a moment that your soul—your higher self—decides to experience lifetimes, or as we said in past chapters, stories, in many different forms. Some may be as men and some as women. But imagine further that in some cases, an individual soul chooses to experience more of these lifetimes in one form than the other. What then happens is that the collective memory of the experience of the soul is such that it becomes more accustomed to the *feelings and sensuality* of one form over the other.

This will cause the soul to have an overwhelming sexual attraction . . . *from the vantage point of that form that the soul has experienced most frequently.* Or in other words, if you have come into this story as a man but you have primarily lived out other stories as a woman, then there is a probability that your energy could be imprinted with the predominant characteristics of a woman—or you might have all of the culturally accustomed characteristics of a male, yet you might find yourself attracted to your same sex.

As a spirit, there is no judgment in this situation because sexuality is regarded as an expression of *spiritual energy,* but as human beings, who are living within the social customs of different cultures, this can become a very difficult situation. This will cause many humans to repress and fight these internal feelings because they are told that it is not socially acceptable.

I am speaking here of the confusion that often arises when *sexual energy*—which is, at its root, akin to creative energy—leaves the unlimited capacity of the spirit and enters into the human physical form. Once this occurs, then the energy becomes limited by the accepted mores of the society in which that person dwells. So should that soul be attracted to another form that is, in this lifetime, of the same sex, then it is considered by many societies to be an abhorrent behavior. But what is actually happening is the true expression of that spiritual energy. I am therefore speaking here of what I would refer to as the *truth* of homosexuality.

There are those who know from a very early age that they have an overwhelming attraction to the same sex, just as most who are attracted to the opposite sex have an instinctual response early in life. There are even those who feel so out of place in their bodies, the current containers of their sexual energy, that it actually causes them to go through the process of changing the physical structure of their form to a different sex. For them, the "Aha!" moment comes when they allow themselves to act in the way that feels consistent with the *truth* of what they feel is their overwhelming sense of attraction and what brings comfort to their souls.

Homosexuality is not an abomination, but rather it is a *truthful* expression of the spirit of a person that is fighting to be seen in spite of the structure of the container. There are times, of course, where any form of sexuality can be learned or a part of experimentation. And again, from the spiritual perspective, there is nothing wrong with however one chooses to freely express one's sexuality. But this is not what I am speaking of when I discuss a *deeper knowing* of your primary sexual *energy*.

Many cultures are coming to understand this at a deeper level, and you are seeing now that more states and countries are moving to accept that the rights of gay people should be recognized and protected. Yet there are many who still try to repress and contain the expression of love into very specific dogma. I have heard the concept that God did not create "Adam and Steve," but rather He created Adam and Eve. In truth, the Creator made everything, and every experience that humankind is dealing with is part of the polarity of energy that the Creator made in order to expand the light. And the light is love, so therefore whatever expands love, in whatever expression or form it takes, expands the love of the Creator. This is not a new concept. Again, it is something that many tribal people, especially Native Americans, knew and followed. The person who had the spirit of both a man and a woman in one body was deemed to be a sacred person. They were protected rather than abused.

"Gay" is a word that, in most languages, came about to describe a situation of happiness. Or if something had a gay appearance, it meant that it was bright and colorful. To be "gay" in society now means that you have chosen to pursue that which makes you happy even if it goes against the social norms—to be *truthful* to yourself. The symbol that the gay movement has come to use is the rainbow. Bright and colorful, the rainbow is all inclusive of every color in the spectrum that the light reflects. This is so appropriate because this is the same way sexual/

creative energy begins—as a multifaceted expression of the light of the Creator.

There are additional complications that might occur in the soul's expression of its sexual energy that go beyond homosexuality. For example, if there is another soul that you have developed a great bond to in other lifetimes, or in the spirit state, you may come across this person in a current lifetime. That bond will be carried over into the human form, and sometimes if you have shared that bond in other stories in a sexual way, then you will seek to share it again. But this person may come into your life when you are already in another relationship. This is often the cause for overwhelming attraction confusion. Often multiple soul mates will incarnate in the same story, and this may be the root of confused emotions and infidelity. Again, the soul does not express love, creativity, and sexual energy in the same context as the physical form, so this can be very confusing and painful for humans.

My point in explaining this information is not to add to the confusion but rather to ask all of you to please refrain from judgment of anyone who is expressing his or her unique sexual identity or the expression of his or her sexual energy. The structures modern society has developed around the expression of sexual energy are very challenging to the sometimes-overwhelming power of the energy.

Clearly I am not speaking here of any sexual activities that are not consensual or are committed on those who do not have the maturity or understanding to consent. Nor am I speaking of those who manipulate the emotions or sexual energy of others by untruths. I am speaking of those who seek merely to be allowed to express the essence of their energy in whatever loving manner they choose.

You will feel no judgment toward yourself of how you express sexual energy when you return to spirit as long as *truth* is the motivation of your actions. But if you are among those who will manipulate others by lies or deceit in the name of love, or who will pass judgment on how another expresses love, then you will judge yourself for this when you return—for you will experience the pain you have inflicted by your actions and your judgments. This is not done as a punishment, but as a tool for deeper understanding and spiritual growth.

Part of the purpose of this book is to help you avoid having to learn these spiritual lessons by illuminating the knowledge that will allow you to live more of your life as a judgment-free human being.

The truth really does set you free!

CHAPTER 10

ONE CREATOR, MANY RELIGIONS, ALWAYS ANGELS

> *. . . in the eyes of the Creator, there is no one true religion. There is no one system that better honors him, if that system sets itself above another system.*

The truth is that there is but one Creator. You have come to call the Creator by many different names, according to the religion that you practice, but there is only one, who answers to all of the names without preference. The Creator set into motion all that currently exists and will continue to exist. We have already discussed the start of creation and the evolution of angels, but I would like to focus a bit more detail on what then transpired.

After the creation of the angels came the creation of the *whole* spirit—the essence of all humans and other forms of creation! This spirit that exists within all of you is also often referred to as the *soul*.

You were created as a slightly denser energetic version of angelic creation, and your form was given the capacity—as with other creatures—to encompass the sexual polarity of male and female genes. This was done so that physical creatures would have the capacity to further create their chosen species.

The original human spirits were not the biblical Adam and Eve. The story that revolves around them was created to give humankind a background into the understanding that there were many who came from the direct design of the Creator but who were all interconnected. There were many souls that were created at the time of what you call the big bang, and these original souls knew everything of the Creator and basked in the light of its pure love. But they were also aware of the energies of darkness.

You cannot create density with light alone. There must be spaces of darkness as well. There must be matter, and there must be antimatter. There must be a positive and negative charge for there to be the electricity that sparks something to experience life. It is what holds everything together. (Again, please do not interpret my use of the word darkness as meaning evil. I speak of darkness merely as the absence of light, and light might also be interpreted as *complete understanding*.)

If they chose to know only the light, souls would not be capable of experiencing the broad gamut of emotions and senses that would allow them to continue to create new experiences for energetic growth. As such, the angel who was the first to be created of the darkness—who possessed the closest amount of all of the knowledge of the universe as the Creator and who you have come to call Lucifer—brought to the newly created souls the opportunity to experience their essence more deeply. He asked if they would allow him to show them the darkness—or more clearly, the absence of light . . . *and this was how the Creator designed it to be!* For if there were no darkness to compare to the light, then what would make one consciously choose one or the other?

How would one appreciate the sunrise or the sunset if there was never the night or the beauty of the full moon? How could one appreciate the warmth of the light if one never felt the cold of its absence? And how could one experience the feeling of love if one never was able to experience its absence?

This was the advent of the creation of *free will* within the soul. The Creator gave you the ability to choose whether you would remain spirits—or choose to become active decision-making creators.

The act of accepting the awareness of darkness was the advent of the soul becoming a "being" rather than just knowing and understanding the light. Knowing the full potential essence of their being, these souls knew that they could not totally be if they did not choose to experience all that was out there, so they chose to let the dark angel show them the absence of the light.

Many writings will say that they were tricked into this, but they chose freely, and this introduced the evolution of the human being into a denser cellular structure, filled with a combination of light and darkness and with the ability to take on any form that they wanted. This soul could live within all forms of creation, from plant to stone to four-legged to crawler to fish to winged ones and finally to the evolving form of mammal known as an ape. This species appeared to have the greatest capacity to exist comfortably in the darkness and the light with the least amount of fear. It also had a huge capacity for expressing love.

Here is where the theories of creationism and evolution meet. As evolution was occurring—in a progression from the animal kingdom—the soul was already expanding through other lifetimes (remember how we discussed that all time is occurring at the same time) and created a human form that was more evolved than those in the animal kingdom. This is why the ape continued to evolve as an ape while the soul created itself in newer, more evolved forms from the knowledge gathered in the *collective consciousness.* Often it has been wondered how man could have evolved from apes while the original primate continued to exist.

You can also see the evolution of the human spirit in animals such as dolphins, whales, horses, and even dogs, which contain much of the human spirit, and this is why they are so compatible with you and have become man's best friend.

In Native American and other indigenous cultures, which I will often refer to because their traditions and legends have remembered many of these connections, it was not unusual for humans to seek out their supportive animal spirit or totem. It was believed that every human had one or more animal guides who would lend their power to help the human through his or her life's challenges. Again, just as I mentioned in the previous chapter about human spirits who have experienced frequent lifetimes as one sex or another, there are those human spirits who, from their earliest days, experienced living in the form of the bear or the dragonfly or the wombat, and that experience was so beloved that the imprint of that energy lives on in their hearts as a very happy and powerful time. These are what are often referred to as your power animals.

Humankind evolved in many forms. Some were consistently close to the form that you are today. Some chose to retain their animal form and evolved within the confines of that creature. Most existed in multiple forms, human and animal and more, because your soul is so much bigger than you could ever imagine in the confines of your physical thinking. Your soul can exist as multiple human, animal, and mineral life-forms at the same time. You are so very much more than you would ever possibly think—until hopefully now!

So how then did religion come to be? As humankind evolved, there existed in the collective consciousness the memory that they had come from somewhere. But the memory of the Creator was clouded by the density of the physical form. Humankind, however, searched for a way to connect with that which gave them light and water and food and the companionship of other creatures. In the search for memory, there were some among them who seemed to have a better connection than others. These men and women were very much human, but had the ability to communicate with nonhumans. They could also see and speak to spirits. This gave them knowledge of prophecy and of healing herbs and other secrets. This was the advent of shamanism—the spiritual leaders and healers of ancient tribal peoples. I am speaking now of those who existed as far back as what you may refer to as the Stone Age. Many of these spiritual leaders also held close connections to their animal spirits so they could communicate with other creatures. The people began to follow these leaders, and they, in turn, taught the people to honor the spirits of all things that brought them life. Offering this honor to an unseen benefactor was the birth of the early days of religion.

From those simple beginnings, religion changed over time. Eventually those who were the strongest in the tribes began to gather more respect because of their ability to protect the tribe or to hunt for the most food. Strength became the currency of power rather than the connection to the spirit, and although the spiritual leaders were still respected, the ceremonies began to change in their focus. With tribal leadership being given to those humans who were the most powerful, then it would only stand to reason that there was a spirit that gave them this power, and they honored that spirit.

And so began the battle of the gods. Each tribe wanted to be sure that it was aligned with the power that would preserve it. So some honored the sun and others the moon and others—still holding some subconscious memory of their connection to animal spirits—began constructing mythical animal gods.

The people would give thanks to their gods in the form of ceremony—as in the past—but when these efforts did not ultimately lead to their winning every battle or having every protection, then the process of sacrifice began. The sacrifice was considered a gift to the gods. In this way, the members would show their devotion and win favor. Some sacrificed animals, and others even sacrificed humans.

At this point, the Creator interceded and called upon the angels to bring the message to humankind that they were all interconnected and loved by one Creator who desired them all to be as one. Thus began the process of angels acting as the manifested messengers of the Creator. You will find stories and legends of the appearance of angels in almost every worldwide religion. We are called by many names, and some are similar in many religions.

In the Hebrew Bible of the Old Testament, there are many stories of God sending angels, and in the New Testament, Gabriel came to announce the birth of a son of God, the Christ. He is also credited by Muslims with helping Muhammad to write the Koran, and there are many references of angels in both the Koran and the Hadith. Micha'el (Michael) has been regarded as the protector of the people of Israel.

The Mormons, in the Doctrine of the Covenant, describe angels as messengers of God and ministering spirits. They believe that their founding prophet, Joseph Smith, was visited by the angel Moroni, who led him to the book of Mormon.

The Baha'i faith speaks of angels and even refers to the "Concourse on High," or the angelic host. Zoroastrianism speaks of guardian angels called Fravashi. Hinduism speaks of *devas,* which are angelic beings, and the early writings of Sikhism makes reference to the angels Azrael, Chitar, and Gupat in their holy texts.

The Brahma Kumaris religion teaches that every member will become an angel of light, and even newer religious movements, like Theosophy, attest to the existence of *devas* who help to guide the processes of the natural order.

Greek philosophers spoke of higher spiritual beings that acted as guides and guardians who would send them answers and advice if they were open to receive the guidance. They would look for these answers in dreams, intuitions, and signs. The word *angel* is actually Greek in origin and means "messenger." However, the word is derived from the more ancient Sanskrit word *angiras* and the Persian word *angaros.*

The Romans taught that each person had a special guardian angel, or *genius,* and would honor this angel on the individual's birthday.

In medieval times and in the Renaissance, angels became the focus of magnificent pieces of artwork that depicted us as being key figures in every important aspect of history and regarded us as being omnipresent in the lives of all humans.

I point all of this out to you in order to make the point that we came here to help different cultures understand their importance to the Creator. We delivered these messages in the languages and concepts that would best be understood by the culture of the times, just as I am doing right now.

There was, however, no time when we delivered a message that any one culture's belief system was preferred by the Creator, nor did we ever say that any one race was the preferred race. We came to sow the seeds of love and interconnection with the hope that hearing the same song, sung by many different voices in many different languages, would bring the world to realize that it was one. But this has unfortunately not always happened.

Religious beliefs are now, as they were in the past, often co-opted into the politics of the world, and just as in the ancient caveman days, there are different nations praying to their God to help them defeat or overpower another nation of a differing belief system. You must realize that this is like someone calling on you to ask that you would allow one member of your family to commit harm to another member of your family—in *your name.*

These false interpretations of our angelic messages are not because humankind is bad or inherently evil. In fact, the true root of the notion of separation comes because of the desire to protect those who are closest to you. But the underlying cause of this sense that you need to protect yourself comes from the most powerful energy associated with the darkness. It is the opposite of love, and it is known as fear.

As the messengers of the Creator, we bring to you the good news that there is nothing to fear. In every appearance of every angel in all holy books, prior to our communication we say, "Fear not," because fear stems from the density of your thoughts and keeps you from remembering your connection to the Creator. We see clearly that fear stems from the thought of being separated from that which you have come to love. Think about it—what is it that you fear? You fear death, which is the ultimate separation from your involvement with your body and this lifetime, which means the people and things you love. Or you fear pain, which is the separation from pleasure that you have come to love. You may fear losing a relationship and have trouble opening your heart for that reason. Or you may fear not having enough money, and as such may not feel comfortable sharing.

Fear is essentially the absence of love. It is one of only two emotions (love being the other) that emanate from your heart center. I appeal to your logic once again. When you love, when you are in love, is not the world a brighter place? Do not the birds sing sweeter, and does not the sky look bluer? And is not every word that comes out of the mouth of your beloved the cutest word that was ever spoken? Think about how you act when you are with a baby; everything the little one does is met with the greatest of love and appreciation because you are filled with love toward that little one—and this is the exactly how the Creator feels about you!

Fear is the reverse mirror image of love, reflecting itself back but from a different perspective. Would you fear the snake if you knew it would not harm you? If all animals were like cuddly little kittens, would you not feel a closer connection to them? We fear that which does not show love to us. We fear that which is different from us. You do not fear the person who looks like you, because you have become accustomed to this. You fear a different religion or culture because it may reject your way of thinking. And you fear that you might not be right in that way of thinking.

When you come to recognize that you are a being of great proportion, and that you are a key part of the expansive creative plan begun by the Creator of all things, it is at first difficult to comprehend. This may be occurring as you read these words. You can feel the connection, but you may not feel good enough to make it directly. Your brain tells you to seek more knowledge to make yourself worthy, so you seek out teachers who will give you more information. Many times those teachers are working within a framework of an organization or brotherhood that was established to draw together those who believed in the same thing, both for companionship and, in older days, for protection.

That is how most of the organized religions came to be. Their purpose was to create a framework for fellowship and to be a safe place where people of like mind could come together to discuss their beliefs without fear of reprisal. Remember that in many cultures, religious beliefs were seen to be dangerous to the state, and so they were repressed.

Differing religious organizations therefore create a place of like-minded comfort for those believers. But the truth, my dear ones, is that in the eyes of the Creator, there is no one true religion. There is no one system that better honors him, if that system sets itself above another system. Just by taking that action, the self-prescribed "preferred" religion dismisses the idea that all creatures are equal in the eyes of the Creator, because all have come from the same source and all are on the path of their own creation.

The goal of the Creator in expanding its energy to create the universe was to expand its very essence into the eternal abyss. It is through the human race that light and dark energies give rise to opportunities to remain in dense energy forms or to cut through the density so that glimmers of the light can shine through. As you grow the light, so, too, does the Creator's original essence grow. And someday it is the design that all energy will again return to pure light—but far larger than the original—and with the expanded consciousness of all that has been created.

If religion is intended to be the bridge between the Creator and the world of men and women, then I come to tell you that you need no church to create that bridge, because you need no bridge. The Creator lives within the air that you breathe, the food that you eat, and the blood that courses through your body. He lives within every living thing, and the more you look within, the more you will realize that you have never been without.

By saying this, I am not encouraging anyone to give up or change his or her religious belief systems, for if they bring you solace and fellowship and a feeling of being closer to the Creator, then they do ignite the light within. I only urge you to begin to realize that the truth of the essence of the Creator lives within you, and above all other forms of creation, you have been given the most exclusive creative tool to become one with the Creator in expansion of the universe: *you have the gift of free will.* You alone are able to evenly experience all of the many facets of light and darkness. As angels we cannot experience this because we have been created as the messengers of one form of creation or the other. We are the messengers of light or darkness. You are far more powerful than you imagine. Remember that there are two basic concepts you can always use to know if you are creating from the light or the darkness. Creating with the light is always expansive. People will grow from this creation; they will become "more than." When creating from the darkness, the energy is repressive and contracting. It is critical, creates the parameters of "better than" or "worse than," and does not allow for all parties to become more of themselves.

Think of this with regard to the way your religious belief system sees others. If it is repressing others, then it is not expanding your way of thinking, and I ask you to remember again:

That which you think . . . is that which you are creating!

The *conscious revolution* is one where decisions that are affecting the collective consciousness of all humankind are actually taking place within the hearts and minds of individuals, and their decisions to act in an enlightened manner are actually shifting the energy of the planet Earth and the universe as a whole.

CHAPTER 11

THE HIGHER
SELF (THE SOUL)

> *. . . you and your soul, your
> higher self, are one and the
> same, and you are regarded
> with the highest esteem because
> you have freely chosen to be
> the gatherers and drivers, who
> continue to expand the essence
> of the Creator . . .*

In the previous chapter, we began the discussion of the grandness of what you truly are. Your essence, that which makes you who you are, is far more profound than your imagination might consider. Some refer to this as your soul, and others have referred to it as the higher self. Many theories have been created to help make sense of its wonder. In this chapter, I hope to offer you a very practical understanding of your very complex being.

Remember that in our discussion of the myth of time, I explained to you that your spirit does not just live on the spirit plane until the time comes for it to enter a body, where it resides until your death. Your spirit is constant and has been there since the dawn of your creation. What you are experiencing is but one facet of its capacity to experience itself.

Suppose for a moment that the Creator is like a master computer. It is the mother (or father) of all computers, and linked to it are millions upon millions of supercomputers that feed information to the master computer, which in turn grows larger and feeds information back constantly through the interaction. These super computers we will call the *master servers,* but we will refer to them by their better-known name, angels. These servers carry information between the master computer and a third level of intelligence, which are the *drivers,* also known as souls. This level of computer is the real work station of the system and drives the creation of new information and data by linking up to billions of data-collection *applications.* These applications take on many forms and may be referred to as humans, dogs, cats, rivers, trees, and so on. But what sets these drivers apart is that they have been given the ability to freely replicate themselves, and they are compatible with virtually every other wireless life form.

The first two levels, the master computer (the Creator) and the master servers (the angels), provide the third level (souls) with universal memory and infinite storage capacity. Let's call this the *universal cloud.* The cloud is very important because the beings (applications), due to the limited size of their container, do not have a great capacity to store memory. That is why they upload memory on a daily basis when they shut down and go into sleep mode. During that time, any memory that is not crucial to the application's function goes into the cloud, where it is stored. Human beings can also call on any of the upper levels for technical assistance at any time. This function is called a request for support from a higher network, sometimes also referred to as prayer.

Those who do request assistance will often experience an upgrade in function and ability to understand other applications, even those that did not work with them in the past. My purpose in speaking to you through this book is to ask you to please request an upgrade! You have the ability to directly interface with any of the collective knowledge that you see as being above you.

In the memory of the *human applications,* there is a "chip" that has given them some limited information about the master computer and the master servers, and humans instinctively know that they can interface with them when they come across situations that are so severe that they could potentially crash. When the human application encounters situations that could cause its local network, or brain, to crash, then those situations may be compartmentalized into quarantined sections of the body. Or if the trauma is too severe, the memory of this information may be sent into the cloud, where it can be accessed at a later time. All memory stored in the cloud can be accessed by the individual who stored it, but it also becomes part of the collective consciousness.

Most beings, however, are not aware that their human applications are being aided by server angels that are aware of all of their design flaws and maximum capacities. They are also not aware that their primary driver, their soul, is running similar applications throughout the universe and has been gathering data that could be really useful to them.

This lifetime or story or incarnation or application, whatever you would like to call it, is all a part of your soul—your spirit—the primary driver that is you! In truth, the names that I have used, which are attributable to the computer world, are so perfectly matched to the world of creation, for the Creator is the master computer, the keeper of all collected thought and function and the creator of the artificial intelligence that came to be known as angels and the rest of creation. I say artificial because it was not the original intelligence. It was a by-product of that intelligence. Again, please do not judge that statement as a lessening of value for us or you, for that is not the case. It is just the reality of what is, and I tell you this in the hopes that you will realize how close you are to the Creator with regard to the process of ongoing creation, and even more important, how much easier your lives would be if you understood that you do have access to information not only from this lifetime and other lifetimes, but you also share a direct link with the very essence of that which created you.

So you see, my dear ones, that you and your soul, your higher self, are one and the same, and you are regarded with the highest esteem because you have freely chosen to be the gatherers and drivers, who continue to expand the essence of the Creator by placing yourself in the firing line, so to speak.

So when we are frustrated with ourselves for our failures, or are excited about our accomplishments, we are actually celebrating them both—for they bring to the collective consciousness the opportunity to expand and to share the information with other souls.

Now, I know many of you are saying, "But Margaret, from the way you are explaining things, it would seem as though people could live in any way that they choose. They can hurt people or be bad people, and they still will be welcome in heaven. Why try to be a good person? Why try to do the right thing? Why be faithful? Why be honest? Why not just forget everybody and look out for myself?" And to this I say to you, in the eyes of the Creator, everyone and every experience is a part of the process of the expansion of the universe, part of the great mystery. Remember that at the essence of your being, you are connected to the source of all love, so your basic primary purpose is to love. It is when an individual being is damaged, or removed from that loving connection, that this person becomes bitter and unkind, and it is then that he or she becomes able to do seemingly horrible things. These individuals come from a place of great isolation from the source of all things, and in truth their actions often cause others, who come from a place of love, to rally to support those who are being treated unfairly; and in so doing, the seemingly evil person causes such an uprising of revolt that this outrage carries into the collective consciousness. In this way, the dark energy actually gives occasion for others to rise above that energy and to cause a greater good and a larger energy of love.

As Gerry writes these words, this is currently taking place all over the world. Despotic dictators who had a firm hold on their countries are being swept from power, and the example of one nation gives heart to another nation to do the same. If there were not that despot, then there would not be that same response or revolt, and the underlying desire of humankind to create an environment of freedom, love, and wisdom would not progress with the same speed.

So you see, dear ones, for most of you it is *not* in your nature to not want to be a good person. The soul is constantly searching for ways to expand the love of the Creator—ways to rise above! You would be amazed to see how, on a daily basis, so many of you choose the path of love and light, even when the other options may be easier. You look deeper and access the higher knowledge.

Sometimes you may wonder, then, why bad things can happen to those good people. Why do they become ill, why do they lose a child, why does her husband cheat and lie when she is such a good and devoted wife? I will tell you quite simply, dear ones, that your soul has chosen these experiences because they bring you the biggest opportunities for your own spiritual growth. Your personal growth expands the growth of the collective consciousness as well.

This is, in essence, rebooting your computer and giving you the opportunity to rewrite the program that is your life. You then have the ability to save the information you desire to save or to discard that which no longer serves your greater purpose. Whenever something traumatic occurs in your life, it is because your higher selves, your souls, are creating the experiences to help each other to grow in love. I know this is a hard concept to hear if you are going through one of those experiences, but, if you can recall that it is your higher self and that of your loved ones who are creating this story, then you will be able to see that there is a purpose to all things.

There is a yin for every yang. There is always balance in the universe, and by that I do not mean that for every good thing that happens there is a bad thing that happens to negate it. But I am saying that there is always a conscious decision to move toward the light or toward the darkness. The more we remember the essence of our creation, the more humankind will turn to that which is most comfortable and loving, which is the original light of the Creator.

"Why," you then wonder, "did the Creator not create the universe in that way in the first place? Why was there need for struggle and war and pestilence and human cruelty? Why were we just not created for the purpose of expanding the light?" If there had only been beings whose purpose was that of expanding light, then creation would have stopped with the angels, and it would have been only a part of the deep vastness of feeling and experiences that have been developed through being. Even if you look at fear, you will see that it is a complex emotion. You choose not to be afraid most times, yet it is fear that helps to protect you in many situations. In some instances, you even choose to feel fear. If that were not the case, there would not be any horror movies or scary amusement-park rides. You choose to experience that fear, because it is within your control, and you know that it is only a story or a temporary ride. You know that it will soon be over, and when it is and you have returned to your real state, it will be something that you came through or overcame. You will feel stronger for it, and maybe you will even laugh at your fear because you have come through the darkness and back to the light.

This is the experience that your higher self, your soul, is going through all the time. It is experiencing the vast array of emotions and experiences you are having and then uploading the information from that experience with insight, forgiveness, compassion, and even levity.

The higher self is constantly striving to find the perfect harmony between the darkness and the light. It seeks the place where the darkness comes to respect the beauty of the light and the light respects the beauty of its shadow.

Do you think it is by accident that the most beautiful times of day are the dawn and sunset? It is at this time that the darkness and the light are at harmony with each other. That allows for the creation of the most beautiful colors and textures, because each is not exerting the full force of its power, but rather acting in concert with the other, forming a beautiful concert of light. And is there a more beautiful sight than the skyline of a city set against the darkness of the night or the beauty of the stars against the blackest sky? Is not the image of the full moon, gently reflecting the light of the sun through the still darkness of the night, considered one of the most romantic of images?

The higher self seeks that level of harmony, and you are a conscious part of creating that within the universe. Just as each droplet of water creates an ocean and each grain of sand a beach, so are you a critical part of creation. Your higher self is creating experiences similar to the droplets of ocean rolling onto those grains of sand. Sometimes the waves are soft and caress the beach, and other times they are strong and carry the beach away with them, but always they act together, flowing in and out, into a greater ocean and finally being absorbed into the sky, into the cloud and the great unknown, where they will again be formed into droplets and rained into new forms to nourish land, to grow plants, to quench thirst, and to continue to expand creation. So, too, are you, my dear little droplets, spreading your essence throughout all of creation. You are the all of the all. You are the way, the truth, and the light. You are the darkest hour that comes just before the dawn. You are the sunrise and sunset, the moonbeam and the darkness of the forest. You are the children of God! *All of you!*

CHAPTER 12

WHY NOW?

> *This is a period where*
> *humankind, and other species,*
> *will become so aware of their*
> *connection to the light that they*
> *will no longer need to grow by*
> *struggling with the duality of*
> *energy and will grow only by*
> *expanding the light.*

So you are probably wondering, *Why now? Why after all of these years of creation, all of history as it has been recorded, is it suddenly so important for humankind to be open to this deeper understanding? And if it is so important, then why does the message not come by way of the heavenly hosts descending to the earth and proclaiming the truth to all of humanity?* Truth be told, this is not a new occurrence; it has all been done before.

Most of the world's religions were begun by prophets who carried the message of the Creator to the world. We would speak to those who could convey our message in the acceptable cultural method to that particular individual group of people. It has resulted in the message (although interpreted somewhat loosely as the years have passed) withstanding a substantial space of time. But while we chose to relay the message to those of modest means and no direct ties to any powerful group, humankind has always chosen to regard these prophets as gods or at least godlike. The messages about the divinity of all of humankind have been greatly lost in translation.

For example, the Bible story of the prodigal son spoke to how the father rejoices when one of his sons returns home, whether that son has toiled in his fields or squandered his money on wine and women. The father represented the Creator, who knows that all experiences will teach those he has created and that all his creations grow from these experiences. The son's coming back to the father represented those who were made by the Creator remembering their roots and being led back to the essence of their being. This was something that the son who toiled in the fields forgot, because he was too busy resenting the other brother for doing what he himself wished he could have done.

You gauge your sense of self-worth, or even your worth to the Creator, by what you do and do not do. This is the internal struggle to "be" in a way that is in accordance with the "greater truths." One of the greater truths is from your field of medicine and was originally penned by Hippocrates, the Greek philosopher. "First, do no harm." In other words, if an act could result in harm for another being, do not take that action. This could also be translated into "Do unto others as you would want them to do unto you." However, the converse to that statement is "do unto yourself as you would do unto others." There are many of you who actually treat others better than you do yourselves, and this is just as harmful as taking an action against another.

The key therefore comes down to your sense of personal "response-ability," that is, your ability to respond in any given situation to that which your higher self leads you to do. And therein lies the answer to the question of "why now."

Most human beings respond to situations based on habit. If you think a certain thing for a long enough period of time, that will become your truth, and those truths that lock you into habitual patterns of doing harm to other things, or to yourself, will *not* set you free! They will imprison you into repeating the same patterns of behavior over and over and over. This will lead you to live your life with resentment or regret.

This affects the overall energy of the planet because there are billions upon billions of you who are doing this at the same time, and each one of you is building the *critical* collective consciousness rather than building the foundation of the *self-loving* collective consciousness. The net effect is that there are billions upon billions of self-loathing individuals who are completely identifying themselves with their faults and who are seeking something or someone who will make them feel better about themselves. And to feel better about yourself, you often need to find someone you are "better than." It might be a group, an individual, or even a nation. This is how people bond into hate groups, terrorists, and even entire nations that thrive on the hatred of other nations.

If individuals were tapped into their higher consciousness, it would allow them to make different decisions, create different habits, and make all of their decisions based on the basic premise of asking, "What will cause the least harm and proliferate the greatest good?"

And so, as much as we have done in the past, angels and other messengers are reaching out to bring this message to the masses. Why now? Well, consider some of the things we have discussed in earlier chapters that are so much a part of the fabric of modern society that did not exist when we delivered these messages in the past. During the times of Muhammad, Moses, Buddha, or Jesus, there did not exist the reality that would allow us to talk about humankind's ability to communicate with others through tiny boxes or to fly in the air like the birds or to overthrow an entire oppressive government by mounting Twitter campaigns! There was no way for them to believe that they had any power to affect a group larger than their family, friends, or maybe a village.

There is an entirely new level of communication among humankind that has never existed before. Technology and science have created wonders that now have people realizing that there is much around them that clearly exists, although it cannot be seen by the naked eye.

The concepts that once were science fiction have now just become science, and that which was fiction now becomes more real by the day. Growing numbers of you believe in something beyond this lifetime, and more and more of you are coming to believe in the existence of other life-forms. You are beginning to recognize that you have done significant harm to the planet on which you reside, and many of you are using your creative and responsible selves to find a solution.

Angels rejoice in this and long to be called upon to assist you in greater ways, because your ability to respond to situations is directly connected to your ability to call forth the most creative and knowledgeable part of your essence, which you now know to be called your higher self or your soul. Your soul has many of the answers you need—most, in fact. The collective souls of all of you on this planet have all the answers to what needs to be done to live in peace, love, harmony, and prosperity—and in total balance with the planet. But to be able to live in this state, you must first be able to access the soul and be able to hear and listen to what you are being told.

Similar to the legend of David and Goliath, you are often presented with difficulties that seem too large to overtake, and you may feel that you do not have the capacity or resources to overcome these "giant" obstacles. But in the story of David and Goliath, the young boy called upon his creative self to trust that a small stone, used in just the right way, could overcome the giant. This is what happens when you trust that you have access to knowing and to solutions that will help you to find the simple answers to complex issues. And you reach that higher place within by changing your own vibration and frequency.

Everything in the universe emits a certain vibration or frequency. These frequencies vary in their vibration and strength the farther you become removed from the light of the Creator. Humans who make every effort to think and act from a place of love, which includes loving and caring for themselves, will vibrate at the highest frequencies. Those who desire to do harm to others will vibrate at the lowest frequencies.

You have all experienced the very clear sensations of being around other people who have such a positive energy that you feel wonderful just being around them. On the other hand, there are those who you try to avoid because they make you feel exhausted when you are around them. This is because you all can *feel* energy. Have you not all felt when someone was looking at you or known when someone was standing behind you? That is feeling the energy of another person. Now imagine that energy is being sent out by several billion people on your planet at one time. Would it not make sense that it would be very powerful if we could help you to learn how to transform your energy into one of those people that others loved to be around? And if a majority of the planet began to act in this manner, can you imagine how powerful that would be?

Up until this point, I have been imparting information that was intended to help you have an overall understanding of the working order of creation so that you would understand the myths that often keep people from realizing that they are so much more than the limited expression they have accepted. I have also explained the truths that have been misunderstood by many well-meaning teachers, thus also holding back the ability for humankind to grow to its fullest potential.

In upcoming chapters, I will speak to you of the specifics that you can do to lift your vibration—the movement of your cellular structure—to put you on the path of that which will help you to be in congruence with your most positive expression of soul. This is not an exhaustive list, and there will be many things that are not a part of the list, but that does not mean other techniques are not good at helping you to grow. My intent is to offer you tools that you could begin to use tomorrow, if not sooner!

This is a period where humankind, and other species, will become so aware of their connection to the light that they will no longer need to grow by struggling with the duality of energy and will grow only by expanding the light.

85

But please understand that your vibratory shift has already begun. By simply reading this book, you have begun the process of a cellular shift. The words I have chosen to use are designed to move your thoughts into a different framework, and in so doing, to begin the process of shifting your thinking.

You were drawn to this book for that purpose, and I thank you for doing so. As more and more of you read this book, the energy will grow stronger, and it will reach the tipping point of critical mass in the collective consciousness that allows a planetary shift in thinking. Change always begins with the thoughts and actions of a single person, and through you it has already begun.

But before we go on to the specifics of how to live powerfully in the present, I would like to expand upon the myth of time and move into the future and how you are already evolving in that time frame.

CHAPTER 13

EXTRATERRESTRIALS & THE FUTURE SELF

> *. . . those who you might actually identify as aliens are but another manifestation of your own souls.*

In the very beginning of this book, I mentioned that many people in your society have a belief that it is only a matter of time until contact will be established with extraterrestrials who will bring to you the knowledge of how to repair your planet and live in peace. This theory has grown over the years and has gained support from many respected thinkers.

Among the current population living on your planet Earth, there is great debate over the existence of such creatures. Some believe that it would be ridiculous to assume that, in the entire universe, human beings were the only intelligent life form. Others believe that life on Earth is all that exists, and that the stories of

UFOs are either just the runaway imagination of a small group of people or the result of secret operations being established by your own governments.

While secret operations of your own governments have been the reason for many sightings of UFOs, I can assure you that there are many life-forms in the universe that have developed cultures far advanced from that which is currently on Earth, and they do connect with this planet from time to time.

What is even more important for you to understand is that those who you might actually identify as aliens are but another manifestation of your own souls.

Remember how, earlier in the book, we discussed the myth of time, and I explained to you that the growth and expansion of the universe, from the original big bang, is still occurring. I also said that when you look into a telescope, you have the ability to see light-years into the past, since that image has taken so long to travel to your vision. Now if that image you are viewing has occurred light-years in the past, then is it not possible that there could be another race of beings that is looking back at you, and you are light-years in the past? That is, in fact, the case!

Those beings that many of you have seen, and the ships they travel on, have come from a part of the universe that would be re-garded as many years in the future, if you still believe in the concept of linear time. In truth, they exist at the same time as you but in a different period of creation. They dwell in a less-dense physical form. As your souls have learned and evolved from the limitations of your current form, they have also learned how to create ships that travel at the *speed of light,* which enables them to actually visit other incarnations of themselves in other time periods.

This might seem complicated, but imagine for a moment that if you had the possibility of going back in time to see how your soul was navigating that period, would you not be curious? There are some modern-day psychologists and psychiatrists who use the process of past-life regression to allow their patients to go past the confines of their minds and open up to deeper levels of informa-tion that are available on the soul level. Most of those who do this type of hypnosis are able to identify traumas or situations in past lives that directly relate to current experiences and behaviors. In many of these cases, the past lives were not famous people, and they were able to be historically validated. Many patients traversed into their soul states between incarnations, and some have even glimpsed at their future selves.

So if you had developed into a race that actually had the ability to go back in time and to see firsthand how you are actively evolving into the being that you had become, would you not do so? That is the reason why future selves have visited your planet in the past and continue to do so to this day. They were the perceived gods who appeared to those who built the pyramids, and they have created many of the natural wonders and crop circles, which are actually energy symbols. They are similar to those used in Reiki and are designed to offer humans more intense connections to the higher self.

Your future selves have, however, chosen to act more as observers over the past few Earth centuries because the inhabitants were not really ready for the information they offered and did not take it in the spirit that it was given, which was to be shared by all peoples. Those who received it either attempted to use it for additional earthly power, or as in the case of the Mayans, once they became aware of a more-developed existence, they no longer wanted to be a part of this world and chose to leave and to live with their more-evolved brothers and sisters.

Most races of extraterrestrials have chosen therefore to watch from afar and only occasionally allow themselves to be more visible. The purpose of their occasional sightings is to offer hope to humankind. They wish to remind the people of the earth that there is something else out there beyond this life experience. They will not assist in the saving of the planet unless a collective, conscious request of the current inhabitants calls on that assistance, and we have yet to receive any indication that humankind would relinquish control of the planet.

Now you might ask as well, "If the stories of aliens are true, then what of the ones that kidnap people and use them for experiments and have left those who remember these experiences feeling fearful and violated?"

To this I will point out that all life-forms, in whatever point of history that you exist, are living either in a mind-set of love or a mind-set of fear. Those otherworldly races that have done these things have not evolved to the point of other future races, and they are not unlike people on your planet who do similar things.

It should not be such a leap to see that there could be future races of people who have not developed spiritually to the understanding that all life-forms from all time periods are interconnected. Even though a race may become technologically advanced does not mean that it still is not living in darkness. Look at your current development on Earth. At the same time that you are developing amazing lifesaving technologies, you are developing technologies that could kill the entire planet.

When one comes to the knowledge that time and space are but an illusion and that all of existence as you know it is intricately interconnected and coming from one source, it becomes impossible to go back to a completely linear way of thinking. This is my purpose in asking Gerry to assist me in writing this book.

If even a portion of the planet begins to take on this shift of thinking, then it will be very possible for a major shift to occur in the future of the planet and the universe.

But the future begins with the actions of the present, one moment at a time.

CHAPTER 14

HOW TO
CHANGE HOW THE
WORLD THINKS

> *. . . focus on a positive reason*
> *for every experience, even*
> *those that you may think of as*
> *negative. . . . It is seeking the*
> *"seed of equivalent benefit" from*
> *all difficulties and believing*
> *that at a deeper level there is*
> *a reason for all things that*
> *happen.*

Now we get into what one of Gerry's clients refers to as the meat and potatoes of this book. We have discussed the myths, we have discussed the truths, and now we will discuss the how-to aspects of actually changing the world.

The simple answer is, of course, that to change what you have you must change how you think. If all thoughts create reality and the current reality does not reflect the thought forms that you have about what you desire in life, then just change how you think! This is, of course, the simple answer—but it could not be more complex!

I mentioned previously that humankind and even the animal kingdom have developed a certain habitual thinking pattern that has evolved as a conditioned response to how situations have transpired in the past. This thinking is difficult to change, because it has become a part of what you refer to as the subconscious mind. The popular thought about the subconscious mind is that it is a portion of the brain that records all the experiences of your life and then, when you are about to undertake a similar experience, the subconscious will remind you of your success, or lack thereof, in the past and will either allow you or stop you from taking that action. Or the subconscious will remember traumatic situations and will bring that to your thinking as a warning.

In fact, the theory of the subconscious is somewhat flawed, because it is not located in the mind at all. Memory is a cellular structure that is stored throughout the physical body, in blood, bone, muscle, and tissue. When you call up a memory, the brain searches for those cells and then will process that information to create a clear picture in your mind, which you refer to as thought. Cellular memory that is not considered crucial to the support of the physical form is then stored outside of the body, within your soul, and becomes part of the collective consciousness.

The physical brain is responsible for all of your conscious actions, as well as the automatic things you do, such as digesting food, sleeping, breathing, and so on. Your brain also will process all of the external stimuli you experience, and it will filter out things that are not essential to complete the program you have established for your survival.

It is very important for you to understand that because your brain's primary purpose is to support your physical form, it may work against you when you try to introduce ideas that it deems as being against its prime directive. Again, if we go back to the workings of a computer, it will function and work perfectly as long as you don't put in information that is incompatible with how it is programmed.

Your thoughts work in the same way. They will be formulated by the parameters of what you understand about your family, your culture, and your current living environment. If you are born into a very poor family, your thinking will be programmed to function within those parameters of thought, and that is why poverty often tends to breed poverty. Yes, it true that there are outside influences that cause people to experience poverty, but what I am speaking of is not lack of resources or opportunity. I am instead speaking of the underlying signals that your brain perceives as the parameters of your expectations to survive. To move beyond the brain's survival mechanism, one must be able to call on the depth of experience of the soul to rewire the brain's thought process and to expand its capacity and definition of survival.

Those of you who were born in what is considered the middle class have generally developed the thinking that your life can be greater than those of the poor if you work hard and struggle to attain success. Often this entails working for another financial class, which is often referred to as the upper class.

Even in the word itself, the underlying tone in the description of this group tells the brain that they are somehow above other people. The upper class generally is comprised of those who were born to members of the upper class; marry into the families of the upper class; or who have developed a beauty, skill, or concept that is so unique that they will be embraced by the upper, middle, and poorer classes. This often occurs in the entertainment and sports fields, and in turn, that person will attain the wealth and status that will allow him or her to become a part of the upper class. The upper class then is comprised of people who have a sense of belonging to that class because they have established the trappings of that status and therefore feel at comfort with who they are. There is a saying, "Money goes to money." There is some truth to this, because those who have money have expanded belief systems about what they need to survive, and as such, they project the energy that draws that to them.

Those who are experiencing an existence within the poorer class often are overwhelmed by their conditions, but many still struggle to move into the middle or upper class. The middle class constantly strives to move past their existence and struggles to move to the upper class. Many even get themselves deep into debt to be able to create the façade of the upper class without actually having the resources or the way of thinking to sustain it.

However, from a soul point of view, there are many reasons one would choose to be born into any and all of the various class structures you have developed on Earth, and many expansive growth experiences come from each.

The class system has a great deal to do with how you think about yourself and your place in this world. It contributes to how you process information, how you see yourself, and your beliefs about your potential to be a catalyst to change the world. Think back upon some of the material that we have spoken about in the previous chapters and you will be able to see how the myth of separation has assisted in creating the roles of class, wealth, and power.

Remember first that all creatures were created by the same Creator and the angels who assisted in the process of creation. Recall as well that the third level of creation was the souls, and these souls (you, the readers of this book) were given the distinct ability to take whatever form you desired by placing a portion of your energy into that form. So you have the ability, and all of you have already chosen, to exist in each of these class states in order to understand and grow from the experience. And in many cases you are doing this in many different forms at the same time.

If that is hard to understand, picture for a moment the online music stores many of you use to download music into your mobile devices. When the music you download from the cloud becomes a part of your device, you now have it in your personal-data container, but it still exists within the cloud for others to call upon as well.

That is how the soul works. It places bits of itself into forms that will allow it to experience life in various data containers, which may actually come in many different races and cultures and classes, all happening at the same time. This allows the soul to upload all of that information from these human devices and applications and to process it into an overall understanding, thus becoming a growing and evolving soul.

In the process of this happening, however, you, the devices, are so busy living your lives that you have no idea that you have it within your collective memory to call upon the experiences of those not in the same groups you are currently a part of. The net effect of this is that *your thoughts about your place in life determine your place in life.*

Now many of you may protest this and say that you did not think yourself into debt or illness and that you are sick of people saying that you are responsible for your hardships in life, and I can sympathize with you for expressing and feeling that emotion. I am not saying that all people are in a place into which they *consciously* put themselves.

You are a part of a greater consciousness or energy that will reflect back to you the things that you think you need to do in order to be loved! I will repeat that because it is very important for you to understand. Everything that you experience in life you do to feel loved by others or feel loved by yourself. Why do you lie on the beach in the sun? Because it is something that your soul loves! So when you do it, you feel good about yourself. Why do you do things for other people? You may feel that it is because you are a good person, and you may well be, but the deeper reason is that it makes you feel good about yourself (self-love), and it may also cause others to love and appreciate you. Please realize that I am not saying that there are not selfless acts; what I am saying is that once you take a physical form, which is denser than your spiritual self, you are partially removed from the light and warmth of the Creator, and you are forever searching for that feeling again!

That feeling is pure love—and that is what you are all looking to experience. Some of you may have gotten yourself into debt while you were trying to take care of someone else or because you were buying things to feel better about yourself. Maybe you never equated it with a desire for that person to love you or that you were always looking for something that would make you feel love for yourself. You see, that is the challenge of the human form.

Often you learn that you are most nurtured or loved when you are ill, when you are angry, or when you are the family peacemaker or caretaker. Those lessons are not things that you consciously think about when you become an adult. But they will affect the things you do as an adult to seek love and acceptance.

We have established that the unconscious mind is not located in your brain, but rather it is the cellular memory that exists in cells throughout your physical form and the energy around you and in the collective consciousness. We have also established that this collective consciousness is the source of all the information you need to have a wonderful and fulfilling life.

Why this is so important to understand is that the memories that are stored *in* your body can often produce physical pain when you are trying to break through to a belief system that may help you move forward. Pain is like an alarm system. It will tell you that there is something in your body that is not working in concert with its survival or with a change in programmed thinking. The problem is that you have become part of a modern society that is more focused on stopping the pain than looking at what the cause of the discomfort might be. And if the pain has not yet created a serious physical condition or cannot be clearly identified, then modern medicine will generally treat it by medicating the symptoms.

So this is then the first step you must take if you are trying to create a better life for yourself and others: *Listen to your body.* It will tell you whenever there is an energetic imbalance that should be addressed. Your stomach might ache, your heart might feel heavy, your throat might feel tight, or you may get headaches. You may notice that you get a pain in your neck when you are tense or when the "pain in the neck" that is causing your tension is around. These symptoms that your body is experiencing are the first indication that the vibration of your body may not be in the flow of what could be bringing you the best possible life you are seeking. Remember that you are, first and foremost, a spiritual being, but you chose to take a physical form to experience intellect, instinct, and emotions as tools to increase your capacity to grow more like the Creator.

Pain will guide you to find where you hold energetic weaknesses, but there is something even more easily accessed that will clearly show you what thoughts are influencing you, and that is your *emotions*.

There are only two overriding emotions, and all of the others are offshoots of these two; they are fear and love. They are the emotional yin and yang of the energy of polarity. When you are feeling love, then you will in turn feel joy, security, passion, and other positive feelings. When you are feeling fear, you will be plagued with doubt, jealousy, possessiveness, greed, and other negative feelings. Fear is essentially the absence of love.

Many of your emotional responses are developed when you are a small child. When children feel truly loved by their parents, they will learn to love themselves. They will be more secure and self-confident, and they will create in their minds the pattern to love others. When children do not feel completely loved by their parents, they begin to do things to get the attention of the parents: sibling rivalry, temper tantrums, pitting parents against each other, and general acting out. When you look at how the children develop, you will often see that they then carry many of these traits into adulthood.

If your first teachers—your parents, grandparents, or siblings— are not completely secure with the fact that they are loved, then you will pick up on their fears. Many children internalize these fears as their own.

But what makes the knowledge of this more palatable is that although you may be currently experiencing patterns that stem from fear, you are also experiencing the polar opposite of love and in so doing are making it more possible to feel the incredible depth of joy and the other wonderful emotions when you move into the energy of love.

So then let us look at three steps that you can take to identify the current state of your energy and emotions and work toward healing the energy of fear and embracing the energy of love:

Step One: Listen to your body. Close your eyes and breathe into it, and picture the breath traveling through your body from the top of your head to the tip of your toes. Notice how your body feels when you do this. Are there certain parts that feel heavy? Are there parts that feel light? Are there parts that feel numb or tingly? Are there parts that feel pain? Identify the feelings and where they are coming from.

Step Two: Identify if the pain or sensation is associated with love or fear. Ninety-nine percent of the time you will find that pain is in some way associated with an emotion that is an offshoot of fear. But occasionally it could be coming from love, like a nervous stomach or heart palpitations. To identify what is going on in a given area, just simply ask your body to let you know what you are feeling in this area, and trust the answers. If a clear answer doesn't come up, then pay attention to what does. See if colors or shapes appear, and then ask your body what those colors or shapes mean. Maybe an image will come up that is symbolic of what your body is feeling. Ask your body what the symbols may mean. The most important thing is to stick with it and to trust your perceptions as your body speaks to you. It speaks to you all the time in the physical sensations you feel. By doing this, you are actually asking your brain to allow those physical sensations to be given a voice and to hear that voice in your thoughts. Your body speaks to you in the same manner that you hear your conscience.

Step Three: If you are feeling something based in fear, place your hand on the area that is affected and imagine it being filled with loving thoughts. Think about the happiest times of your life when you have felt loved. This doesn't have to be another human's love. It could be the love of a pet; being overcome by the beauty of something in nature; or something that was so strong that it left you recognizing that there was some wonderful divine order, which *is* love.

This may not be easy to do when you first get started, but it does get easier, and soon you will find that you are doing it almost automatically. The key is that you need to be able to very quickly find something that reminds you of feeling loved. This can sometimes be challenging, because your cultures, and certainly your news reports, are so conditioned to focus primarily on the bad things in your life that so often the good things are taken for granted.

In keeping with that challenge, I suggest that you begin to keep a small pad, which we will call your *gratitude guide*. This is a place where you can write down all the things that have happened to you in that day for which you feel grateful. Again, in the beginning this may be difficult because of how much most people take for granted.

You can begin to change this by mentally keeping track of your actions as you go through your day. Did you awaken to your alarm clock? Did you see that as an annoying reminder of another day? You could see it as a blessing. It is another morning that you have opened your eyes to the sound of something that was created to help you not to miss your important appointments. In most cases, your clock is powered by electricity that flows into your home through the labors of other people. You may think, *Yeah, but I pay for that power.* This is true, but would you not feel more wonderful about yourself if you knew that somewhere there was someone who was thankful that you were going to work to do your job? Give thanks for those who see to it that you have electricity.

Let's go into the bathroom now. At one time in history, not even the wealthiest and most powerful individuals could go into a room and switch on internal lighting while they adjusted hot and cold water faucets to create the perfect personal temperature for their bathing. Not to mention the fact that there are still places in the world where homes have no running water or indoor toilets. You can be very thankful for that little room and the people who made your soft towels and shaving cream and deodorant—all things that make your life easier.

Is there heat in your home or fans or air conditioning? Up until the 1950s, many homes didn't have these things. Most needed coal stoves to heat their water and for single-room heat! When you leave the bathroom, what do you do next? Do you change into the clothes that were made for you by someone else? Did you ever give thanks for that person or for the person who designed the clothing that you feel so pretty or handsome to be wearing?

Did you eat breakfast? Was there food in your kitchen that you picked up from a store, a one-stop location for the creation of a meal? Did you ever give thanks for the people who work there or the people who farm the food, ship the food, or even package the food so it will stay fresh for you?

When you head out to work, do you drive, take a bus or train, or bike? Did you ever give thanks for the people who built your form of transportation or for the shelter it gives you in the elements? In the case of public transportation, did you ever give thanks for the people who drive you?

When you get to work, do you ever give thanks for your job? Many people are without jobs. And if you are one of those who does not have work, are you grateful for being healthy enough to seek it elsewhere?

If you are in a relationship, do you love and appreciate and give thanks for that person? If you are not, do you give thanks for those who try to fix you up because they see such good in you?

If you are going through an illness, do you give thanks for all the wonders modern science has now created and for the myriad of alternative healing modalities that are available? Do you give thanks for your health if you are not ill?

My point is that if we really look from a place of love, there is so very much to be thankful for, and these are the things that you should write in your gratitude guide. There is also a secret to gratitude. Have you ever given a gift to a person and he or she was so grateful that it made you want to get even more for that individual? Alternatively, have you ever given a gift to someone who responded slightly or not at all? Didn't that make you think, *Why did I bother?*

Do you remember how we discussed that like energy attracts like energy? If you are grateful for all you receive, even your challenges, you will attract to yourself even more things for which you will be truly grateful. But in the converse, if you have no gratitude for that which you receive, you will put forth the energy that you don't need anything, and that is exactly what you will receive.

If you want to change your thinking from a place of fear to love, you need only to catch yourself when you are thinking something that stems from lack or ingratitude or fear and replace that thought with something that makes you grateful.

Preferably this would be something that really hits an emotional chord and makes you recall the feeling of joy it gave you, which will elicit a true feeling of gratitude. All people have had an experience in life that makes them smile when they think of it—something really good that happened! There was a time when you felt deeply loved or appreciated by others or had an amazing experience that made you feel so fortunate! This thought will become what I will refer to as your pivot thought. You can use that thought, or any other one that gives you the same emotional response, to pivot from a fear-motivated emotion, like anger, to a loved-based feeling of joy or gratitude.

Please, I ask you to not, for the sake of debating this principle, say to me, "But Margaret, what if my fear is valid? What if someone has a knife and is about to stab me? If I think a happy thought, will that help?" While I am sure that in the greater picture your happy thought would change your energy from fear, there are times for which the fear response was originally created: to stimulate the survival instinct of fight or flight when a physical danger is present. That response allows the body to create all of the reactions that are necessary to function at that moment. This was part of the divine order, and it exists in all creatures to some extent. The difficulty is that this very important psycho/physiological reaction can be going on all day in the body of someone who is stressed about work, a relationship, or health issues. The net effect is that the body becomes exhausted by constantly producing internal chemicals that should be reserved for a true survival situation. So in this non-life-threatening instance, yes, a positive thought that stimulates an emotional response of happiness can help to slow down or stop the fear response.

At this point you may be thinking to yourself, *That's it? That's the big truth of what I should do to change my thinking? All I have to do is think a nice thought?* I can already sense the chuckle in many of your throats and the doubt in your minds, but let me reiterate what I said in the very beginning of this book: *To change the world, you must change the way you think, one mind at a time, one moment at a time, and one thought at a time! And you are already creating the thoughts that are creating your current life!*

Catching yourself in a moment of negative thought and pivoting to a positive, happy, or grateful thought also begins to stimulate another very powerful force that cannot only change your own thinking and experiences; it can also join forces with other like-minded people to create an energetic shift on the planet. This energy is called *faith*.

When I speak here of faith, I am not speaking of it as one might understand it for a particular religion. I am rather speaking about the belief in a deeper connection that is related to your current existence on this planet. It is a focus on a positive reason for every experience, even those that you may think of as negative. It is seeking the "seed of equivalent benefit" from all difficulties and believing that at a deeper level there is a reason for all things that happen.

Faith, then, is the belief in the unseen. It is the belief that no matter what one may experience, something better is coming. If you are now able to accept that this existence is only a small component of the immense size of your soul, can you see that faith—the belief in something bigger than your current experience—directly ties your thoughts to your soul, your angels, and finally to the Creator itself?

How this can change the world on a practical level is another interesting phenomenon:

- One person changes his or her thoughts from a fearful thought to a faithful (focus on a positive experience) thought.

- That person begins to change his or her habitual thought patterns by doing this as often as fearful thoughts come up during each day.

- Within a 21-day period, the process of replacing a fearful thought with a faithful thought begins to create itself into a new form of habitual thinking. It is true that a behavior that is consistently repeated over a 21-day period begins to ingrain itself into the human psyche as a habit.

- Other people begin to notice a change in the person who has shifted his or her thinking. They are drawn to this individual because of his or her positive attitude. They feel the difference in the person's energy and eventually begin to mimic the behavior of the positive person because they seek the same happiness that he or she is experiencing.

- As more people begin to do this, then the habit of positive (faithful) thought begins to take root as a movement in the collective consciousness, and at a given point, a tipping of thought begins to move from the fearful end of the spectrum to the faithful.

As the collective consciousness shifts, then the movement of thought begins to accelerate at a very quick pace, because it is now all downhill. If this sounds impossible, then I would offer to you the example of the ant in the insect kingdom. An ant is able to lift many times his weight but not for extended periods of time. The ant will move a needed item for a certain period of time, and then it will rest or place the item in a safe place until it is able to come back. Often another ant from that colony will pick up the item where the first ant left off and carry it to the next place. Ants are most often not aware that they are picking up their loads from another that has already carried it; they are simply moving what they have found from that location to the next.

It is the same in the human experience. Picture the faithful thought as a heavy boulder that you are pushing uphill, trying to bring to the valley that your family lives within. You intend to use this boulder as part of the construction material for something new you are building. The boulder is heavy, and you are used to just leaving boulders this large, because it is the collective thought of your tribe that it is just too hard to push the boulder uphill. But one day you begin to change your thinking about the situation, and you push the boulder just a little bit every day. You get to a certain point and say, "Hey, I got farther than I thought." You begin to tell others about your new way of thinking or they notice you acting in this different way, and they ask you, "Why are you pushing the boulder uphill?" You explain to them how you got much farther than you ever thought was possible, and they decide to push also. Soon you have assistance from the most unexpected places. Finally the boulder reaches the top of the hill and one of the new thinkers decides to give it a slight nudge over the tipping point, and suddenly the boulder takes on energy of its own and begins to speed its way into the valley. The people in the valley did not work to get the boulder there, but now they know that they have to get on board with this new way of thinking, because they have no choice; they can make room for it, or they will be crushed by it.

And so, the single person who began the task of moving the boulder, a little bit every day, actually gave birth to an entire movement that changed the way people behaved. This is the very way that all of the current religions of your world began. Single people, then small groups, and then larger groups began to follow certain beliefs; and as more people saw their commitment to this thinking, they began to join in. Eventually, even the governments who worked to repress these religions realized that they had to make room for this new way of thinking.

But religion is not the only thing that is affected by faith. If you think this is a far-fetched concept, then please look for further proof in the tech world around you. Two individuals changed how the world functions with the invention of the personal computer, and everything that followed has changed how we live and work. A couple of key people were instrumental in the creation of Facebook, which has changed how the world communicates.

This is why the power of individual thought is more important now than ever before. A single person now has the ability to share his or her thoughts with the planet, simply with the click of a mouse. Now there are single individuals in different parts of the world who have begun citizen movements via social media that have started the momentum of a boulder of free thinking to come crashing down on dictatorships and other governments that would not get out of the way of the new thought. It is happening every day, all over the planet. The thinking of one person is creating a new concept of faith in new possibilities, which is changing the face of history.

What is happening at this time is that a single individual's thoughts can combine with other individuals' thoughts so quickly that major changes are happening on your planet on almost a daily basis. Remember again, like energy attracts!

Revolutions rise and are quashed. The world feels positive about itself and monies rise, and then the slightest change will cause a loss in consumer confidence (translated: fear) and entire economies will crash! Things are happening at a faster pace than they have ever happened, and this is because of your ability now to communicate your thoughts with everyone else on the planet in real time. Your thoughts are being communicated everywhere on Facebook, Twitter, and the most powerful of all for creating emotional response, YouTube. It has been said that a picture is worth 1,000 words, and I would say that a video that creates emotional response is worth 100,000 words, because it creates many new thoughts in a specific belief that are powered by visually inspired emotion. When you couple this with the power of music, you now have the perfect thought storm.

This is why changing your thoughts from fearful thoughts to creative, positive, faithful thoughts is so crucial at this time. You are being barraged by the thoughts of others every day. Some may be spreading those of divisiveness. Some may be spreading those of racism. Some may be spreading those of hate and destruction. There need to be many, many voices that are speaking of unity. There need to be voices that believe in the inherent goodness of the human spirit and the relationship of that spirit to the energy of the planet. Those who consciously choose to think in this manner will be participating in moving thought to only the most positive of places.

I promise you that as you slowly move that boulder uphill, one thought at a time, you will find that there are like thinkers who will help you push the boulder while you are resting, and then suddenly, you will find that there are many like thinkers who are supporting you in pushing that boulder of thought. Then suddenly you will see that your thought has tipped and is now gaining momentum and growing in size as it picks up more and more supporters as it races downhill. The key is to continue to create these positive thoughts so that, as they cross over the tipping point, they will join with other positive-thought boulders, and eventually the valley will be re-created with bedrock of positive, creative, and faithful thoughts.

It only takes a single moment to change your thinking, but that moment will change your life!

There are other ways as well to change yourself and the planet, and many of these ways will make it possible for you to more easily shift your thinking. These methods will literally raise your energetic vibration so that you will send out a frequency that will attract to you like-minded people and situations that will make it possible for you to follow your bliss.

CHAPTER 15

RAISING THE VIBRATION OF THE PLANET

The time has come! . . .
The energy of the original
one is in all things. . . . The
time is now to embrace not how
we are different but that we
are the same.

The process of changing your daily thoughts can be difficult at times, because many of your habitual ways of thinking can be so rooted in your body or outside of your body. So to raise your level of thinking, it would be helpful for you to learn some special things to change the vibration of your energy field.

Every being has a certain frequency that is its unique "phone number" or "address," if you will. When you are operating at full energetic capacity, your number operates like a very clear phone line that can easily receive information from your soul. If fear is causing you to limit your experiences or thoughts, then your signal becomes weaker and weaker and you may actually lose the signal to good things that are being transmitted to you. We have all experienced this. When you are functioning at full capacity, you are always at the right place at the right time, but when your signal is clouded by fear, then you can't seem to "catch a break." There seems to be more month than there is money, or you find yourself just missing opportunities or choosing not to do things that you find out later would have been wonderful.

There are certain techniques that can help you to raise your personal signal or vibration. The ones I am recommending are not only very powerful, but they also all share the common thread of being able to be universally learned and self-administered. You can do this for yourself, and you can share them with your loved ones.

Before I begin to speak of the specific techniques, however, let me take a moment just to touch on what exactly you feel like when your vibration, or energy level, is running at optimal capacity.

When your energy field is working optimally, you feel confident and good about yourself. Things seem to flow in an effortless manner. You feel a sense of lightness and happiness and gratitude. You attract wonderful people and experiences to you, and in general you find that you are just on top of the world. Many of you may not remember experiencing this feeling, or if you did, you can recall it only from your childhood years. For others, you may have noticed similar feelings in the very early days of a relationship when you felt totally in love with someone and this feeling was reciprocated. For some it occurs at the birth of a child, when they are struck by the total purity and innocence of the little one they hold in their arms.

This is a wonderful feeling, and it is what you have the capacity to experience a majority of the time. What cause you to lose this feeling, however, are the stressors in your daily life that you begin to give more power over you than they rightfully deserve. How many of you have experienced the feeling of job stress, financial stress, health stressors, or relationship stress, and as you are feeling these things, you just can't seem to find a way to get past the energy you are feeling? There is a reason for this.

Imagine yourself as being a clear glass filled with pure water. Your energy source begins just like this, and it is ideally how you could potentially exist. Sometimes your life begins to fill with denser energy, which you might picture as oil being added to the pure water. First the stressors are light, similar to clean oil, which you can see through, but they are still displacing the perfect balance of your pure water (energy). Then heavier energies begin to fill your space, which you might picture as thick, dark oil. Now you can't seem to see the purity that you started with. As the oil pours into the container, it will displace the water, and then it will float to the top, creating a film over the water.

That is what is happening to your energy, or if you prefer, your vibration or life force. It begins as a crystal clear pool, and then it becomes weighted down by ideas and concepts that don't mesh or mix with the original creation. These particles of emotions and thoughts do not blend with each other, so they sit on the surface, creating a barrier that makes it hard to see through, or if the energy is heavy enough, it will displace the original energy from the container, filling its place instead with a heavy muck, if you will.

Can you begin to see how you are experiencing this in your own bodies? Fear and love are like the oil and water; the two can live side-by-side, each having its own purpose in the mix of life, but they do not mix together. When love is the major energy, it will dissipate fear, and when fear is the major energy, it will dislodge and displace love.

So in order to raise the vibration of love, it is necessary at times to focus on finding the energy that is clouding the pure, original energy or locate the energy that has been forced out by the substantial intrusion of the heavier energy.

Virtually all of the energy we are talking about has occurred in your past and very frequently during your youth. This was the time when you were formulating your thoughts about how you would come to see the right and wrong in the world. For the most part, however, adults do not see that the patterns of behavior they currently struggle with may well have begun in their youth. The body remembers the situations that caused you to structure your first beliefs, such as, "Nobody ever said life was going to be easy" or "Money is the root of all evil" or "That person is not like us or not good enough" or "You are not in the same league as those people."

These are the thoughts that form your early opinions, beliefs, and fears. And most are buried somewhere in the cellular memory of your body.

To find and release these memories, there are several techniques that are very successful and that can be done in the privacy of your own home, most with little to no cost. I am stressing this because for the planet to undergo a major shift, it is imperative that many people have access to this information. And while some of you who are reading this may have heard of these techniques, there is a great majority who are learning many of them for the first time. For more information on all of these techniques, as well as cutting-edge experts in each field, you can go to Gerry's site: **www.gerrygavin.com**.

Here are the techniques that I recommend you look into. Some of you will feel more attracted to some than others, and that is part of your unique nature and free will. Allow your gut feelings and your heart to draw you to the methods that just feel right for you. You could also choose to do all of them so that you can make your decisions based on your personal experience. There is no wrong answer in this regard.

And if you are not sure, I would suggest that you submit a request to receive technical assistance from the program developer. In other words, pray. In Old English, the word *pray* was synonymous with "ask": "I pray thee, kind sir, could you show us the correct path to take?" Your prayers are the same. You are simply asking the Creator to help you to find the correct path. One additional note about prayer is that in the process of being sent to the Creator, your prayer automatically is uploaded through the collective consciousness. When more than one person is praying for the same thing, those prayers join energy and forces. Prayer is a very powerful energetic tool, and it is a healing technique and a positive creative technique. The Creator hears and answers your prayers by allowing you the access to all the energy you will need to meet your request if only your belief in your prayer is strong enough to stay firm on the direction. The first and quickest way I would tell you to raise your vibration and those of others you love is to:

Pray

For yourself, for those you love, for those who anger you, and for those you do not even know.

By directing your prayer for yourself, your loved ones, and strangers, it confirms the belief of the equality of all of humankind and gives greater power to your prayer, because your intention is to not only increase your own personal vibration. You are petitioning to increase the vibration of those you love, you are sending love to those who anger you, therefore dissipating the anger, and finally, you are sending energy to those who may most need it and allowing the Creator and the angels to spread this to an almost-infinite group. This is very powerful indeed!

Meditate

There are more people who meditate now than there have ever been, and this is a very powerful process as well. What makes meditation different from prayer is that you can easily go into it without a request or agenda. Your entire purpose is to quiet your mind and allow yourself to go into the stillness of your being where you will be able to have a direct connection with your higher self or soul.

Meditation can take many forms, but all of it originates with your breath. By focusing on your breathing, you allow your body and brain to fill with more oxygen, which causes a relaxation response and allows your mind to quiet from its thoughts that are fueled by fear. Gerry uses and teaches a very simple breathing technique that he refers to as the lucky seven breathing process. It is a very easy exercise to do.

You just sit or lie down comfortably and count your breathing. Inhale to the count of seven (about one second apart), and then hold your breath for seven seconds. Then exhale for seven seconds and continue to repeat this process. You will come to a point where you are no longer thinking about anything and your mind is just focused on the breath and the count, until eventually you just begin to focus on the breath alone and then the calmness and the clarity of thought that comes into you. It is best if you can breathe in through your nose and blow the breath out of your mouth—if that is possible.

There are those who believe you should go into a meditation session with a question or problem you wish to resolve while you are in the process. This is fine to do and can be very productive, but I would still suggest that you go into meditation as often as possible without any particular agenda other than relaxation and enjoyment. It is in that state where you will most increase your vibration, and this will allow you to come out of your meditation with a mind-set that will help you be open to solutions for your life. You can do this at home, at work, or virtually anywhere, and it takes no substantial training. As you become more proficient at meditation, you will find that it takes you less time to induce a relaxed state, and you will actually look forward to that time spent.

I encourage you to take short breath breaks throughout the day, especially early in the morning before you start your day or at night just before you sleep. These are both very powerful times, as they give you the ability to set your day up for success and in a relaxed state; or, alternatively, you can use the time to dispel the day's stress and enter your sleep state in a carefree manner.

For many who see meditation as an "out there" sort of idea, I would like to point out that many hospitals, particularly those specializing in cancer treatment, offer classes in meditation to help put their patients in the right mind-set to support their bodies' healing efforts. It has been scientifically proven that the brain-body connection can be totally affected by the mind-set of the patient, and since it is powerful enough to build up the body's vibration for healing purposes, then clearly it is powerful for other purposes as well.

Experience and Learn Reiki

Reiki is one of the most ancient healing techniques in the world, and it is all about increasing your vibration. It does this by allowing you to be tuned in to the frequency of information that is being downloaded and the universal life energy that is sent out directly from the Creator, the angels, and your soul for the purpose of health, happiness, and unconditional love. This is the same method that was used by the ancient Egyptian priests and other worldwide nationalities. The work *Reiki* is a Japanese word that means "universal energy or life force," and it directly connects you with the flow of energy between the spiritual world and the physical world. Currently, the primary way of being attuned to receive this energy is through another person who has been taught to become a master of the art and science of Reiki. This attunement can take place both in person and over great distances, and we have aided Gerry in discovering methodologies to do so over distances. Like other things I am describing in this section, Reiki can be self-administered or you can do Reiki on other people, animals, plants, foods, and even on the energy in your workplace. Since it amplifies healing and creative life force, Reiki is safe for everyone. The other wonderful aspect is that when you are performing Reiki on someone else, the energy is passing through you and into that person, so you are also receiving healing and creative energy that lifts your vibration!

The best way to understand what I am talking about is to experience Reiki firsthand. You can generally do this by attending a free Reiki Sharing in your local community. Reiki practitioners often do these to share the knowledge and the wonderful feelings that Reiki produces.

Learn about Tapping
(Also Known as Emotional Freedom Technique)

For those of you who are reading this and live in the Western world, you may find comfort in the concept of tapping. This technique links together the Eastern technique of acupressure with the Western concepts of talk therapy. It centers on using your fingers to tap on identified acupressure points on the head and upper torso and speaking out loud about the situations in your life you are trying to overcome. Giving voice to your feelings in this manner is very productive because it tells the body to release a specific energy that you may be holding in your bones, muscle, or tissue. This energy of a past memory or trauma not only stays locked within these body parts, but it also replicates itself every seven years. When you loosen the energy and bring it to the surface, it may feel bad at first, but the more you focus and stick with it, the more you will find that your body is actually talking to you by identifying pockets of held energy through heaviness and sometimes even slight discomfort.

Tapping is a wonderful tool, because you can teach it to yourself or use the assistance of an instructor, and you can use it for helping to release all types of energetic blockages: physical, emotional, and even spiritual. This technique will greatly raise your vibration as it breaks through your blockages, and I believe there is no coincidence to the fact that, again in your linguistic phrases, you tend to say that you tapped into something when a discovery or insight is made! I wholeheartedly advise everyone to learn this technique. There are many already using it, and it has great potential to help with the global shift in thinking. There is also a wonderful film that was created about tapping called *The Tapping Solution*. Its creator, Nick Ortner, along with siblings Jessica and Alex, also support a program aptly called Tapping Angels, which seeks to get free *The Tapping Solution* films to prisons and other community groups.

Essential Oils and Energy

One of the strongest senses that both humans and other animal species have is the olfactory sense—the sense of smell. You know how the smell of a particular perfume, food, or natural fragrance can take your mind back to crystal clear memory of when you smelled that before. Just as we discussed the importance of breath when we were discussing meditation, the nose also allows breath to carry powerful messages. It is your olfactory sense that identifies pheromones, which are some of the most powerful triggers of attraction between members of the animal kingdom—including humans. Trees, plants, and flowers produce all of the healing remedies humankind and the animals need to be healthy and to vibrate at the right frequency for them to be connected to their souls. Indigenous people learned about ways to use plants, bark, and flowers to heal them by watching the animals do the same. Many of these plants create natural oils that can be inhaled, rubbed on the skin, or sometimes even ingested. You are probably already aware of many of them. The smell of lavender can now be found in many shampoos and candles, and people have come to accept that this is, in fact, soothing. Orange is now used in cleaning solutions, but it is also wonderful at lifting emotions. Pine and peppermint also have very strong healing properties. The former is used to kill germs and bacteria, and the latter is very well known for helping to cure stomach concerns. So the concept of using oils to help you to raise your vibration may not seem like such a strange one after all!

The truth is that essential oils can become one of your most trusted friends. There are oils for your first-aid kit, for your bath, for your thinking, and for your food, and all will contribute to your overall well-being. Native Americans and other indigenous peoples understood that everything around us—the trees, the plants, the flowers—held a special energy and life force, and they would respectfully utilize that force to feed and provide medicine for their people. At the end of this chapter, I will speak a little more on the energy around indigenous peoples.

In these modern days, you can purchase oils from many good companies that are dedicated to maintaining the purity of essential oils. Some of these oils can be found at health-food stores or online, and many even create blends of oils that can be used for very specific purposes. There are also wonderful practitioners who can help you to learn about the oils, both online and in your communities. Essential oils are a fast and easy tool to lift your vibration and frequency, and that is because they are in complete alignment with nature and the purity of the essence of the plant, flower, or bark. I urge you to look into them!

Develop Your Intuition

Most people have heard about, or even experienced, different aspects of what has come to be called the sixth sense. You have also become very comfortable with the term "women's intuition" when it comes to women often sensing things that men, with their more logical approach, often miss.

But both men and women can develop their ability to see beyond the limitations of the five senses and to embrace a deeper knowledge that will allow them to download information from a greater vantage point.

There are wonderful teachers who can instruct you as to how to develop your intuitive skills. This is a part of the human capacity that only a few experience, and yet it is a skill that all of you have the ability to possess. Just like Gerry, you can learn to talk to your angels as well as other spiritual helpers and the Creator himself.

In the upcoming years, as the energetic frequency of the planet increases, those who have the ability to be more in touch with their intuitive side will fare much easier.

Learn to open your third eye, your sixth chakra, and you will see the world and yourself with a clarity that you never thought possible.

Soul Retrieval

You may recall that when I was talking in an earlier chapter about how your body processes energy and trauma, I mentioned that there are times when your brain, similar to a computer, identifies a situation as being a "mandatory delete" item. This would be like your computer bypassing the quarantine file and sending information directly to the trash without even giving the body the chance to review the contents. In the parlance of those who work with this phenomenon it is called soul loss, because a portion of the energy that your soul has invested in your human form is literally separated and remains in another place and time.

While there is not yet a technique for bringing soul pieces back on your own, Gerry is in the process of researching how this can be accomplished. He has been performing soul retrieval for years and teaches it to others in workshops. He also performs long-distance soul retrieval. Soul retrieval is performed by someone who practices the ancient shamanic art, whether in your home, in their healing space, or over distance. For many people this technique helps every other technique to be much more powerful. You cannot heal parts of yourself by utilizing the other techniques if there has been significant soul loss. I would liken it to having a party where the guests of honor have not been invited. Soul retrieval allows you to bring back pieces of your soul that may have been lost in some of your most formative or transitioning periods.

"Afformations"

Several months ago we led Gerry to discover an online educational program mentored by its visionary founder, Jeffrey Howard. There were many wonderful faculty members in this program who carried angelically inspired messages. One of those was Noah St. John, who discovered a system of changing the way you think and ultimately your vibration. This system is called *Afformations*. You know that many times throughout this book I have used analogies relating to computers and technology, because it is something that so many of you are familiar with. Noah was inspired by this same concept and came to realize that the problem most people have with their thinking was that they were asking the wrong questions. He realized that your minds work just like Google— they are search engines. When you ask a question like, "Why do these things always happen to me?" your mind will respond, like a search engine, and will call up all of the cellular memory it can find to directly answer the question and prove the theory of why you are deserving of certain things happening to you.

Noah wondered what would happen if you changed the search by *changing the question*. Rather than saying, "Why can't I ever get ahead?" you would ask, "What about me makes it so easy for me to get ahead?" In this manner, similar to entering a different question into your search engine, the brain will look for cellular memory to find a different answer. It will call on strengths and experiences that will help you to retrieve not only memories but also the emotional feeling of the energy from those successes.

There are times when affirmations alone are not always successful. It is sometimes difficult for your brain to believe a concept that is totally alien to your current life circumstances. If you are telling yourself that you are prosperous when you are sitting in a darkened house because your electricity has been turned off, it is a hard concept for your brain to accept. But if you ask, "Why is it so easy for me to earn the money I need to be prosperous?" then your brain is set to work searching for the answer to that question, and it will help you to call to mind or to bring up the energy of everything that will help you create this reality. This is a very powerful technique that Gerry has been using and sharing with his clients as well. There is more information about Noah St. John and this technique on Gerry's website. Dear ones, I cannot stress enough how powerful a tool this is! Please begin to allow this to help you in your life today. When used in conjunction with affirmations, it is even more powerful.

Going Back to the "the Way"

Throughout this text there have been references to indigenous people. I do this because for most of the people who lived on the lands of the earth, before they became "civilized," they had a genuine love, respect, and protection for all of life. When settlers came to their lands, most indigenous people greeted them as friends and shared all they had with them. Their belief systems taught them that conscious living was not just a catchphrase one might work on to develop oneself. To them it was a way of life. The land was respected and revered as a miracle of the Great Spirit or other spiritual benefactors. The creatures, great and small, were all treated as brothers and sisters. There was no green movement because conservation and protection of the planet were part of everyday living. They allowed their intuitive eyes and ears to open so they could hear the language of plants, water, the wind, other creatures, and the world of spirit.

The time that is moving toward us is a time to go back to this way of living. Gerry often uses the phrase, "Everything new age is really old school," and in the case of the beliefs of the indigenous peoples, this is so very true.

It is time for all people to look back and learn the ways of the original people of their countries. There are many elders who stand ready to teach those who ask how to save this planet and how to live with respect and compassion for all creatures. They speak languages that come not from the throat but directly from the heart, and I urge you to learn them and to learn how to speak from the heart. If one lives the way or follows the good red road, that will increase one's vibration and capacity to love and to be a part of the healing of the planet.

The time has come! We are all one—all of us, from the Creator to the angels to you human spirits to the animal spirits to the rock and stone and water and air. The energy of the original one is in all things, and all of this energy weaves through every particle of matter in the universe! The time is now to embrace not how we are different but that we are the same. Like many different fashions of color and tone and style, which are all cut from the same amazing and wonderful fabric, you are all my relations and each other's as well!

There are scores of other healing techniques I have not elaborated on in this section, simply for the purpose of brevity. Yoga, Pilates, and tai chi are wonderful methods to connect body, mind, and spirit. Massage and other forms of body work will allow you to release tension and loosen cellular memory as well.

Remember that once you make the decision to live your life in a more conscious manner, you will be empowering your angels, your higher self, and the Creator to lead you to those techniques that would be most helpful. Again, it all comes down to your decision-making process. What you think will be what you create!

The future of the planet rests with your thoughts. You are empowered beyond your belief. Starting today, think only thoughts of the world you would like to create, filled with love, abundance, joy, and peace!

CHAPTER 16

EVERYTHING
IS IN THE SPACES

> *Space is the illusive God particle
> that everyone is looking for,
> and you have access to it every
> moment of every day and all the
> spaces in between!*

Recently, Gerry had a young woman who came to him for a private reading. She was asking him to reach out to me to help her overcome a struggle she was having with very obsessive-compulsive thoughts in dealing with her relationships with men. She said that her thoughts seemed as though they had a life of their own—like a freight train that would just take off and keep going without stops until she felt as though her mind was going to finally derail and she would just go crazy.

As I began to respond to her comments, I asked her if she noticed that in her thinking she would have one thought that would jump to another and then jump back or to another new thought.

121

To this she said yes, but still the obsessive thought would always come back. To this I responded that the place of change—the place where she could grab back control of not only her thoughts but her life as well—existed in the space between her thoughts. This space is where you are literally holding the remote control of your mind and making the decision as to what program you are going to continue to watch!

Have you ever noticed that sometimes as you watch TV or scroll quickly through things on your computer or phone that you are surfing between many different avenues of information and are looking for something that is going to catch your interest? When you find that thing you desire to look at or listen to, you will then give up the search for a bit of time. Even if you are a person who will watch a picture within a picture on your TV, there is only one item your mind is able to focus on at one time. You may believe that you are multitasking on many things at one time, but there is always a transition period—a split second where you make the decision to move your thinking from one item to another.

That space is the space that connects you to your soul and to the very essence of all that exists! When you are in the space between thoughts, you are essentially in the space between cells of thought. You are in the invisible territory scientists have studied and argued over for decades. You are accessing the substance that interconnects all things—the very matter that holds all things together and attracts particles to each other to form substances, first from a thought and eventually to a solid matter. The space between thoughts is connected to the same matter that creates the space between all other things, from the tiniest atom to the vastness of the stars in the heavens and the darkness that surrounds them.

The space between your thoughts is actually much larger than you might imagine. It is close to 90 percent of the matter of thought cells. Many of you may have heard scientists estimate that humans only uses 10 percent of their brain matter, but that is not entirely true. Your brain is constantly functioning, and all of its parts are working. It is just that you are only focusing on 10 percent of what your brain is doing, and the other 90 percent is made up of energy that holds everything else together. These spaces are primarily made up of magnetic energy that binds cells together and causes matter to move about. What I am essentially saying is that the space between your thoughts helps them to form and then sets them into motion.

Imagine it this way: when the blades of a fan begin to turn in a circle, they set particles of energy in motion. You do not see any of these particles that are called air, but the motion of the fan pushes the air outward, causing a breeze. You will actually feel the particles of air, invisible particles to your eye, touching your face and moving your hair or clothing. Nature does this in a similar manner by setting larger groupings of particles in motion, and the result is called wind. Particles move together in a certain direction and then bind to other particles, and motion is created.

Your brain does the same thing. You are watching a program on TV, and then a commercial comes on and you begin to surf the stations. A program catches your interest, and you begin to watch it. Soon you are focused on the new story, sometimes so much so that you forget that you were watching the first story. This is how your brain works with your thoughts. You are thinking on a certain thing until something distracts you or interests you, and then your thoughts move in a different direction. This is how most people think, and there is so much external stimulus now that you are constantly being barraged with information that grabs your attention. The problem here is that so much time is spent being distracted to new thoughts that there is little time for your mind to spend in *constructive thought*. Constructive thought is thought that actually allows you to tap into the spaces between your thought cells so you can begin to create the *energy in motion* (e-motion) that will create the thoughts you are thinking. Very creative people get very emotionally connected to their creative projects, and it is that e-motion that sets energy in motion around the thoughts and allows them to be created at a faster pace.

Remember that we discussed that the matter that exists in the spaces is *magnetic energy,* and back in the very beginning of the book we discussed the *law of magnetic resonance.* When you can catch your thoughts in between the spaces or can direct your thought to think with *focus* and not with random *thought surfing*, then you will be shifting your thoughts from the 10 percent of your brain to the other 90 percent, which will allow you to expand the magnetic resonance of your thought. In other words, you will create a signal that will be set in motion and sent out to the universe—where it will connect with like thoughts and come back to you.

Your creative thoughts act in the same manner as a boomerang; the more energy you put into them, the farther you can throw them and the faster they will come back to you!

But if you are still having trouble understanding the importance of the spaces to your thoughts, I would ask you to read this next sentence: Iftherewerenospacesin yourthoughtsthenyouwouldfindyourselfalwaysthinking withnobreakandnowaytotellwhereyourthoughtswere beginningorwheretheywereendinganditwouldbeverytiring.You maybeabletofigureitoutbutittakesyoualotmoreenergyanditisvery veryverydifficultbutassoonasyou allow the spaces to enter the picture, then it is as though you have taken a breath and now every word, just as every thought, becomes clearer and jumps out at you!

Without the spaces between words and even the punctuation that you have developed to help you to separate your written words, your ability to read would be much more challenged, and it would not allow you to read in the almost automatic way most of you do.

This is the same for music. When you think of music, particularly the beat of music, it is the rests that give music its power. If music were nothing but random notes that were constantly playing with no pause, then every melody would be constant and redundant. But changing the melody and the speed by placing spaces between the notes and allowing notes to bend and fade creates the passion and the amazing healing quality of music. The power is in the spaces between the notes. The spaces are what hold the whole musical composition together.

Gerry does shamanic healing work with the use of what he refers to as *shamanic drumming.* It is very powerful and helps his clients access much deeper healing in less time. The drumming consists of a single-frame drum, which is playing a very steady one-note beat at about two or three beats a second. Scientists have found that a steady drumbeat of this type creates a trance state to occur in which the brain waves alter into a higher state of consciousness and all four quadrants of the brain work in unison. Gerry had always believed that it was the drumming that created this state, but it is really the spaces between the drumbeats that connect with the spaces in the person's thoughts. The drumbeat causes the brain to increase the size of the space between thoughts, and it allows the person to go into that sacred space where he or she can grow, learn, and heal.

You could also think of the spaces like the spaces in a piece of fabric. While the fabric might look solid, it is actually fibers that are woven around spaces that give it its ability to be strong and yet flexible. When you think about a down coat, it is actually the spaces between the fabric and the feathers that protect from cold and fill with warmth. The spaces transmute the energy of the elements.

So we can see that powerful spaces exist in many things in nature. I could go on for pages and pages about natural phenomena that are caused by the spaces between matter. But how does this relate to the young woman who came to see Gerry for assistance with her problem, and how will it help you?

Slowing down your thinking and directing your thoughts gives you the ability to alter obsessive thoughts. When you are having obsessive thoughts, it is because your brain has reduced the cellular structure of your thoughts and you have less space between your thoughts. The space is still there, but it seems like it isn't because it is being filled with the thoughts you are most trying to resist. Those obsessive thoughts to which you are giving the most attention cause the brain to give more power to them, and they are therefore magnifying and repeating themselves more often and filling the spaces. In other words, your magnetic resonance is attracting the same thoughts or memories of similar past thoughts or new experiences that will reinforce the old way of thinking. Sometimes medication actually causes the brain to short circuit this process, which allows you to manufacture more space between the cells, and this is what causes a relaxed state and less obsessing. For others the same results can be achieved by meditation.

I hope you are beginning to see that everything we have discussed in the earlier chapters has been crafted to lead up to this chapter and the clear understanding of how important it is to recognize that you are creating your reality and for you to *create more space*. This is why people usually feel more relaxed when they go away to the mountains or the seashore. The more open your spaces, the more open your thoughts can be. But you can just as easily create open space in your thoughts by practicing some of the techniques we have discussed throughout the book.

Remember, dear ones, that when you think with gratitude, you widen the spaces in between your thoughts because you become focused on what is good in your life, and gratitude is an expansive energy.

When you catch your negative thoughts, acknowledge them, and let them pass, replacing them with positive thoughts and empowering memories from your past, you are pivoting your thoughts and creating new ones, thus expanding the spaces.

When you meditate, pray, do Reiki or tapping, stimulate your senses with massage or aromatherapy, dance, laugh, and express love, you widen the energy of the spaces within you. And when you perform Afformations, you literally expand the spaces by empowering them to grow in their magnetic capacity to bring expansive, noncompetitive, effortless, and powerful energy to your energetic space. All of these things will help you to expand your space within.

Space is not just something that you see up in the sky. It is something that exists in you and around you and is a part of everything. Space is the illusive God particle that everyone is looking for, and you have access to it every moment of every day and in all the spaces in between!

AFTERWORD

When you are attempting to create a book that is intended to help humankind reimagine everything it has ever known about life, there are many questions that will come up.

This book was not intended to be the all-encompassing text on how to best navigate the coming years. It was intended to get the ball rolling, so to speak.

There have been wonderful books written over the past few years about the power of intention and the law of attraction. The problem has been that many of the people who have read these books were not able to move forward with the concepts because they continue to see themselves as limited beings, and then they come to doubt the advice because it is coming from a fellow human. We are hopeful that by engaging in the direct dialogue of an angel with humans, we can keep this conversation going, and in so doing, we can continue to offer support, guidance, and of course, love!

The thing that one must understand is that angels have been entrusted by the Creator with the job of providing assistance to you only upon your request.

As I mentioned earlier, by reading this book you are, in essence, creating a request for assistance, which then allows us to amplify the energy in your lives so that you can better experience those things that will help you to raise your vibration. By doing this, you add to the energy of the planet. You might think this seems far-fetched, but consider this for a moment: Imagine that you are playing the radio or TV in your house, and the volume is amplified to its maximum potential. That would create a loud message coming from your house or apartment. Now imagine that others in the neighborhood hear what you are broadcasting, and ten more of you begin to play that same station at that same volume. Now your neighborhood would be filled with that same program. Other people who can hear it faintly from your location will get curious and will tune in so they can hear it better, and soon a large enough group is listening to the same thing and it becomes a trend or a hit or a blockbuster movement.

To quote one of my favorite sayings I hear humans often use, "This is not brain surgery!" It is something that seems so very simple, but that is because you have become so very used to complicating your lives in so many different ways.

Several years back there was a saying that went, "Everything I know about life I learned in kindergarten." Its basis was that you teach your young ones things like sharing, playing nice, not making fun of another, and learning about your differences, and if you still lived by those simple truths, your lives would be so much easier.

I have come to bring to you some complex concepts that have at their root a very simple truth. It is possible for us all to live as one. Peace is possible, health is possible, worldwide love is possible, the end of poverty is possible, the healing of the planet is possible, and discovering that we are *all* the sons and daughters of the Creator is possible. And all of it begins by going back to some very simple thoughts—the same ones you teach the littlest among you—and recognizing that your thoughts create everything.

This is only the beginning of our conversation. I have asked Gerry to continue my opportunity to speak to you through the blog that you will find on **www.gerrygavin.com**. There you will also find the link to the Facebook page that will let you post any of your questions. I have also asked Gerry to arrange for public gatherings and web gatherings where you will all be able to ask further personal and global questions so you will be able to feel the depth of these truths in your heart and soul. You will also be able to find information about all of the vibration-raising techniques I discussed in the previous chapters, along with individuals who work closely with Gerry in this endeavor.

I look forward to meeting all of you who are reading these words, to speaking to you further through Gerry, and to hearing your joys and concerns. I also hope that you will reach out to meet and converse with your own angels, who would love to create a deeper communication.

Remember, think about the world you would like to create, for that is exactly what you are creating!

Go in peace.

All my love,
Margaret

ACKNOWLEDGMENTS

Behind every book there is a boatload of people who help to make it a reality. They may be directly involved with the creation of the book—or they may be the people who provided the love, care, and support that enables the author to pursue this endeavor. There are so many people I would like to thank that I am sure I am going to forget someone. But here it goes . . .

I have already dedicated this book to you, but I thank you, Gail, for bringing me to all of the people, places, things, and ideas that directly or indirectly formed who I am today. Many say that behind every successful man there is a woman, and in my case it has clearly been you. All of my successes are yours as well. You continue to influence me every day—and I relish each one, just to see what you have in store!

But before I met Gail, there were two other women already in my life, and although they may credit me with raising them, I credit them for growing along with me. A father could not be more fortunate than to have two daughters like Tiffany and Melissa. You went through some very rough times but grew into women, wives, and mothers who have wonderful hearts, senses of humor, and character, and I am so proud to be your dad. I will never forget cleaning the house to Earth, Wind & Fire and Steely Dan or bridging the generations when we rocked out at Grateful Dead shows together. I know that angels watch over you and my wonderful grandchildren, Ian, Ryan, and Kyla, who extend your love into the world and into my heart. I love you all so much! To John Greene and David Medina—it's hard for a dad to watch a new man come into his daughter's life, but I know that you two will always be there to offer your love and support. For this I love you and entrust to you a wonderful family.

To my mom and dad, Julie and Tom Gavin, you have crossed over, but I know you support me from the heavens the same way you supported me in life. You were the most wonderful parents, and Tom, George, and I thank you for the life you gave us and the inspiration and courage you brought me that led me to writing this book. To my aforementioned brothers—you both taught me so much about life. When I look at most of my qualities, I can see clearly that I learned them from my big brothers. I love you both, and I extend that love as well to my brother Jim. You joined our family later in our lives but have brought it so much love and joy that it feels as if you were there from the beginning. Thank you guys! To my sister-in-law Judi Gavin, you left us way too soon, but we will never forget the love you brought into my brother Tom's life and into all of ours as well. You were such a special person, and we miss you dearly! To my niece April-Anne, you always made me feel like a hero, and you made the name Uncle G-Rod something that will always make me smile!

Along the way I was fortunate enough to be adopted into another family who made me feel so welcome in their home. So to my "adopted" daughters, Amanda and Courtney, and grandchildren, Max and Sarah, thank you so much for making me feel so special, being so supportive, and sharing your lives with me! I thank you for making me a part of cheerleading practice, shaved heads, beautiful theme parties, and inspirational writing. Vinny Emmolo, the newest member of the tribe, thanks for helping me get control of the TV for at least one football game per season and for always making a funny joke even funnier.

And while I am acknowledging adoptive family members, there are two who have brought amazing joy to my life.

David Anderson, there is just no one in the world like you. I just say your name, and I have to smile. You are bright, funny, loving, caring, and an amazing artist. To me you are like an angel that is just waiting to burst out. Thank you for everything you do and everything you are. And to Dot Yurkiewicz, the teenage Brahma bull-riding rodeo cowgirl turned overprotective mom and grandma—I loved you like my own. Thank you for being my supporter, friend, and second mom. Heaven became a little more fun on the day Dot Cole walked through the gates.

Ted Kozick, in life you always urged me to do this work, and you believed in me long before I believed in myself. Since you have crossed over, there are just too many amazing things that have happened for me not to believe that you aren't pulling some strings in support of us all. You taught us all that all you need is love. My thanks go out to you and to Pat, your wonderful wife. I am honored that you called me brother. And I am equally honored to have a sister like Doris O'Donnell, who brings an extra boost of joy to every family occasion. You and your husband, Tom, love to be part of an interesting conversation. I hope this book will make you proud and will kick off some of those conversations.

A special thanks to Barry and Jean Yurkiewicz of the Bar J Café, the official caterers of *Messages from Margaret*. Your amazing cooking and great humor gave me food for both body and soul. I am lucky to have you as family, friends, and neighbors.

To my teachers along the way who provided encouragement, inspiration, and knowledge in many forms—Lanee McLaughlin, Albina Godlewski, Joanne Rossi, Susan Ruth, Black Elk, Michael Harner, Sandra Ingerman, James Redfield, Neale Donald Walsch, and Ted Andrews. Most recently I was extremely inspired by the work of Jeffrey Howard and Christine Kloser, who have created two amazing spiritually based training programs intent on changing the mind-set of how people do business and ultimately change the world. I was brought to you when the time was right, and I hope that I can bring many more your way.

My humble thanks go out to my very patient spiritual guides, Margaret, White Feather, and Metume, who have guided me through the most amazing experiences. Never in my wildest imagination did I see my life unfolding in this wonderful and mystical way.

To my friends who have supported this endeavor in every possible way, the official Gerry's Angels: Tara Arnold, Michelle Ruhmann, Chris Olsen, Grace Anastacio, Patricia DeFazio, Grace Poli, Doreen Messina, Kathy Wager, and a very special thanks to Preston "PJ" Bergen and Don Burkett. This book would not have been possible without your support.

Thanks to my editor, Megan Finnegan, who patiently corrected my grammar and helped these channeled words to flow more smoothly—all while she was only days away from her wedding! Lesley Siegel, my thanks for the wonderful design of my website and for all of your help in everything digital and then some. And special thanks to my daughter Tiff, who could be a book editor and who provided much-appreciated, eagle-eyed, post-production editing assistance.

Thank you to my book promotion intern, Magdalena Burnham, and to a very special person and publicist, Jill Mangino, who guided me to Balboa Press and inspired me to get the word out. And to her assistant, Ginger Price, for working so hard to set up press and radio interviews and always being so positive! Sandy Powell from Balboa Press, I thank you for all of your assistance, guidance, encouragement, and excitement.

To Karen Noe, my fellow Balboa turned Hay House author, thank you for all of your support and sharing the excitement of this experience with me. And to Siobhan Hutchinson, thank you for bringing Margaret and me to so many new people and for all your faith and support!

To the early-morning and late-night drivers of Academy Bus Lines who made the ride smooth enough that most of this book and its corrections were actually written on the daily Jackson to Manhattan commute.

For Ariel and Shya Kane, who have successfully aided thousands of individuals and couples to be here in the moment and who provided the radio moment that brought Margaret to the attention of Hay House, I send you the warmest thanks. And a special thanks to Alexandra Gruebler, our London Hay House angel, who took the book under her wing, and with the assistance of Marion Bardou and Monica Meehan, is spreading Margaret's words throughout the world.

And of course, to the team at Hay House: Louise Hay, who authored the first self-help/healing book I ever read and who had the vision to create such a transformative company; Reid Tracy, whose leadership took that vision to an international audience and proved that you *can* have a successful corporation that actually is based in integrity; and to all the other wonderful people who brought this book to market in record time: Margarete Nielsen for being the glue that holds all of the complex parts of this wonderful company together; Shannon Littrell and Patrick Gabrysiak for making the book even better and for making the editorial process organized but still fun; Christy Salinas for great creative direction and Tricia Breidenthal for the beautiful cover and interior design; the wonderful Hay House marketing and web team: Gail Gonzales, Heather Tate, Darcy Duval, Donna Abate, Dani Riehl, Wioleta Gramek, Melissa Brinkerhoff, Muni Syed, and Diane Ray; publicist Erin Dupree; sales director John Thompson and national sales manager Arron Alexis for getting the books everywhere; and Shannon Baum, Stacey Smith, and C.J. Juarez for being so helpful with the business end of being an author.

I hope I have remembered everyone! My heartfelt thanks to all of you!

ABOUT THE AUTHOR

For over 20 years, **Gerry Gavin** has been working as a communication and empowerment specialist, helping individuals to reach their full potential by teaching them how to listen to their bodies, minds and spirits. He does this through a combination of modern-day alternative therapeutic techniques and ancient shamanic practices.

He is a workshop facilitator, speaker, life coach, medium, energy-medicine practitioner and the creator of the very successful *Angels and Shamans* workshop, which puts participants in direct communication with their angels and guides.

Gerry lives on a small horse farm in New Jersey with Gail, David, their Australian shepherds, Wyatt and Annie, and about 30 other wonderful farm critters.

For more information on classes, workshops, private readings with Margaret, shamanic services and event listings, please visit Gerry's website.

www.gerrygavin.com

NOTES

NOTES

NOTES

NOTES

HAY HOUSE TITLES OF RELATED INTEREST

YOU CAN HEAL YOUR LIFE, the movie, starring Louise L. Hay & Friends
(available as a 1-DVD program and an expanded 2-DVD set)
Watch the trailer at: **www.LouiseHayMovie.com**

THE SHIFT, the movie,
starring Dr. Wayne W. Dyer
(available as a 1-DVD program and an expanded 2-DVD set)
Watch the trailer at: **www.DyerMovie.com**

THE ANGEL WHISPERER: Incredible Stories of Hope and Love from the Angels, by Kyle Gray

THE ASTONISHING POWER OF EMOTIONS: Let Your Feelings Be Your Guide, by Esther and Jerry Hicks (The Teaching of Abraham®)

CONVERSATIONS WITH THE OTHER SIDE, by Sylvia Browne

INTUITIVE STUDIES: A Complete Course in Mediumship by Gordon Smith

MESSAGES FROM YOUR ANGELS: What Your Angels Want You to Know, by Doreen Virtue

THE SPIRIT WHISPERER: Chronicles of a Medium, by John Holland

All of the above are available at your local bookstore,
or may be ordered by contacting Hay House (see next page).

We hope you enjoyed this Hay House book. If you'd like
to receive our online catalogue featuring additional information
on Hay House books and products, or if you'd like to find out
more about the Hay Foundation, please contact:

Hay House UK, Ltd.,
292B Kensal Rd., London W10 5BE
Phone: 44-20-8962-1230 • *Fax:* 44-20-8962-1239
www.hayhouse.co.uk • www.hayfoundation.org

Published and distributed in the United States by: Hay House, Inc., P.O. Box
5100, Carlsbad, CA 92018-5100 • *Tel:* (760) 431-7695 or (800) 654-5126 • *Fax:*
(760) 431-6948 or (800) 650-5115
www.hayhouse.com®

Published and distributed in Australia by: Hay House Australia Pty. Ltd.,
18/36 Ralph St., Alexandria NSW 2015 • *Phone:* 612-9669-4299
Fax: 612-9669-4144 • www.hayhouse.com.au

Published and distributed in the Republic of South Africa by:
Hay House SA (Pty), Ltd., P.O. Box 990, Witkoppen 2068
Phone/Fax: 27-11-467-8904 • www.hayhouse.co.za

Published in India by: Hay House Publishers India, Muskaan Complex,
Plot No. 3, B-2, Vasant Kunj, New Delhi 110 070 • *Phone:* 91-11-4176-1620
Fax: 91-11-4176-1630 • www.hayhouse.co.in

Distributed in Canada by: Raincoast, 9050 Shaughnessy St.,
Vancouver, B.C. V6P 6E5 • *Phone:* (604) 323-7100 • *Fax:* (604) 323-2600
www.raincoast.com

Take Your Soul on a Vacation

Visit **www.HealYourLife.com**® to regroup, recharge,
and reconnect with your own magnificence.
Featuring blogs, mind-body-spirit news, and life-changing
wisdom from Louise Hay and friends.

Free e-newsletters from Hay House, the Ultimate Resource for Inspiration

Be the first to know about Hay House's dollar deals, free downloads, special offers, affirmation cards, giveaways, contests, and more!

 Get exclusive excerpts from our latest releases and videos from *Hay House Present Moments*.

 Enjoy uplifting personal stories, how-to articles, and healing advice, along with videos and empowering quotes, within *Heal Your Life*.

 Have an inspirational story to tell and a passion for writing? Sharpen your writing skills with insider tips from *Your Writing Life*.

Sign Up Now!

Get inspired, educate yourself, get a complimentary gift, and share the wisdom!

http://www.hayhouse.com/newsletters.php

Visit www.hayhouse.com to sign up today!

 HAY HOUSE

HAYHOUSE RADIO
radio for your soul

HealYourLife.com ♥